vegetarian
cookbook

the vegetarian cookbook

Over 200 delicious ideas for brunches, lunches, suppers, picnics, family meals and entertaining, all shown step-by-step and with 800 fabulous photographs

Editor: Linda Fraser

southwater

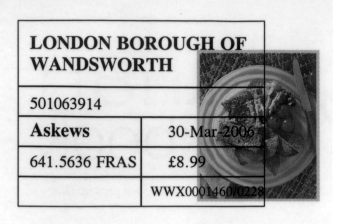

This edition is published by Southwater

Southwater is an imprint of Anness Publishing Ltd
Hermes House, 88–89 Blackfriars Road, London SE1 8HA
tel. 020 7401 2077; fax 020 7633 9499
www.southwaterbooks.com; info@anness.com

© Anness Publishing Ltd 1998, 2005

UK agent: The Manning Partnership Ltd, 6 The Old Dairy, Melcombe Road, Bath BA2 3LR;
tel. 01225 478444; fax 01225 478440; sales@manning-partnership.co.uk

UK distributor: Grantham Book Services Ltd, Isaac Newton Way, Alma Park Industrial Estate, Grantham, Lincs NG31 9SD;
tel. 01476 541080; fax 01476 541061; orders@gbs.tbs-ltd.co.uk

North American agent/distributor: National Book Network, 4501 Forbes Boulevard, Suite 200, Lanham, MD 20706;
tel. 301 459 3366; fax 301 429 5746; www.nbnbooks.com

Australian agent/distributor: Pan Macmillan Australia, Level 18, St Martins Tower, 31 Market St, Sydney, NSW 2000;
tel. 1300 135 113; fax 1300 135 103; customer.service@macmillan.com.au

New Zealand agent/distributor: David Bateman Ltd, 30 Tarndale Grove, Off Bush Road, Albany, Auckland;
tel. (09) 415 7664; fax (09) 415 8892

A CIP catalogue record for this book is available from the British Library.

Publisher: Joanna Lorenz
Managing Editor: Linda Fraser
Project Editor: Sarah Duffin
Designer: Bill Mason
Illustrator: Anna Koska

Previously published as *Get Fresh: Deliciously Different Vegetarian Dishes*

1 3 5 7 9 10 8 6 4 2

NOTES
For all recipes, quantities are given in both metric and imperial measures and, where appropriate,
measures are also given in standard cups and spoons. Follow one set, but not a mixture, because they are
not interchangeable.
Standard spoon and cup measures are level.
1 tsp = 5ml, 1 tbsp = 15ml, 1 cup = 250ml/8fl oz
Australian standard tablespoons are 20ml. Australian readers should use 3 tsp in place of 1 tbsp for
measuring small quantities of gelatine, cornflour, salt etc.
Medium eggs are used unless otherwise stated.

Front cover features Leek Tart, an adaptation of Asparagus Tart with Ricotta (page 240) - simply substitute chopped leeks for the
asparagus and braise them in a little butter for 10 minutes before arranging in the pastry shell.

CONTENTS

INTRODUCTION
6

SOUPS
18

STARTERS
38

SALADS
64

SIDE DISHES
88

LIGHT LUNCHES
132

SUPPERS
164

SPECIAL OCCASIONS
220

INDEX
252

Introduction

WHETHER FOR HEALTH REASONS or due to ethical concerns, more and more people are rejecting animal products and turning instead to a vegetable-based diet and realizing that there is life after meat, after all. With the plentiful supply of fresh vegetables, fruit, herbs, nuts, grains, pulses and pasta that is available to us, the possibilities of creating really exciting and varied recipes have never been greater.

It is not only vegetarians who can enjoy vegetarian food. The fresh, light and innovative recipes that have come to the forefront of new-style vegetarian cuisine provide a tempting departure from many of the heavier, non-vegetarian dishes. This book gathers together some of the best recipes in the world, all of them packed with fabulous tastes and textures.

You are what you eat, and we are constantly being urged to choose a diet rich in complex carbohydrates found in cereals, grains, fruits and vegetables, which are abundant in vegetarian cooking. If you include dairy products in your diet, restrict your intake by choosing skimmed or semi-skimmed milk and low-fat yogurts and cheeses. By limiting the use of oils to unsaturated types such as olive, sunflower, corn and peanut, you can reduce the level of fat in your diet considerably.

With options for everything from light snacks to special occasion dinners, every recipe here is delicious proof that eating the vegetarian way is not only nutritious, but entertaining and exciting too. Try them and enjoy them.

Fresh Vegetables

Thanks to the range of fresh produce now available, the choice for vegetarians has expanded enormously.

Asparagus
Asparagus spears have an intense, rich flavour – delicious served with melted butter.

Aubergines
Differing in colour and shape, aubergines have a smoky flavour when cooked.

Beans
Broad beans, green beans and runner beans can be steamed or lightly boiled in salted water until *al dente*.

Broccoli
Quick and easy to prepare, broccoli can be eaten raw with dips, or cooked.

Cabbage
There are many varieties of cabbage. Care should be taken not to overcook this vegetable.

Carrots
Carrots have a sweet and fragrant flavour. They are just as delicious eaten raw as they are cooked.

Cauliflower
Cauliflower has a pleasant, fresh flavour.

Celeriac
Celeriac has a hint of sweet celery.

Celery
With its distinctive flavour, celery is an ideal ingredient for soups.

Chillies
Members of the capsicum family, these can be very fiery.

Courgettes
These are succulent and tender with a delicate flavour.

Cucumber
This has a crisp, refreshing taste.

Fennel
A crisp, delicious aniseed-flavoured vegetable.

Garlic
These firm, round bulbs have a very distinctive flavour.

Leeks
A versatile vegetable with a subtle, oniony flavour.

Lettuce
There are many varieties of lettuce available. Most salads include this vegetable.

Mushrooms
Whether cultivated or wild, mushrooms are an essential ingredient for vegetarian cooking.

Onions
Onions come in many different varieties. They can be sautéed, roasted or eaten raw in salads.

Parsnips
A sweet root vegetable with a distinct earthy flavour.

Peas
Sweet tender peas are unbeatable. Make the most of them when they are in season.

Peppers
Green peppers have a fresh "raw" flavour whereas red, yellow and orange peppers are sweeter.

Potatoes
Rich in carbohydrate, potatoes can be baked, boiled, fried, sautéed, mashed or roasted.

Pumpkins/Squashes
These have a fibrous flesh with a mild, slightly sweet flavour.

Shallots
These small bulbs are ideal for using in sauces.

Spinach
Rich in iron, spinach can be eaten raw in salads or cooked.

Swedes
These are ideal for adding to soups and casseroles.

Sweetcorn
Eaten on the cob with salt and a little butter, sweetcorn is absolutely delicious.

Tomatoes
These come in a variety of sizes and form the basis of many vegetarian dishes.

Turnips
Sweet and nutty flavoured, turnips range from very small to large, mature vegetables.

Dairy Produce

Both local and imported dairy products are now widely available. Most have low-fat versions.

Butter/Margarine
Butter is a natural dairy product made from cream. Margarine is a butter substitute made from vegetable fat.

Buttermilk
This is skimmed milk with an added bacterial culture, to give it a natural tangy flavour.

Cheeses (hard and semi-hard)
Hard cheeses are often essential for cooking and of course Parmesan is an important ingredient for many dishes.

Cheeses (soft)
Cottage cheese, curd cheese, mascarpone and ricotta are all soft, moist cheeses used in many dishes. Other soft cheeses of culinary note are mozzarella and tangy feta.

Cheeses (blue)
Blue cheeses such as gorgonzola, Roquefort and Stilton are among some of the most popular cheeses used for sauces, soups and tarts.

Cream
This is available in many forms including single, double, clotted, whipping, soured and crème fraîche.

Eggs
Rich in protein, eggs are used in both savoury dishes and desserts.

Fromage frais
A creamy, fresh white cheese sold in pots.

Milk
This is available as skimmed, semi-skimmed and full-fat, as well as condensed, powdered, homogenized and evaporated.

Quark
This soft white cheese is made from fermented skimmed milk.

Yogurt
Yogurt is available in various forms including organic, low-fat, Greek and bio.

Pulses and Lentils

Pulses and lentils are a good source of protein. Both need to be washed, and pulses should be soaked overnight before cooking. Beans should initially be boiled hard for ten minutes to destroy their toxins. Do not add salt until they are nearly cooked as this toughens their skins.

PULSES, BEANS AND SPLIT PEAS

Black-eyed beans

Sometimes called black-eyed peas, these are the only beans that do not need soaking.

Butter beans

These are ideal for soups or pâtés as they have a velvety texture.

Chick-peas

These round, beige-coloured pulses have a strong, nutty flavour when cooked.

Haricot beans

These are small, white and oval. They are ideal for slow cooking, as they absorb the flavour of herbs and spices easily.

Kidney beans

Kidney beans are dark red-brown beans with quite a strong flavour.

Green and yellow split peas

These tasty and nutritious peas are ideal for thick, hearty soups and are used in Indian cooking.

LENTILS

Brown and green lentils

These small lentils have a delicate flavour and retain their shape during cooking. Green lentils have a slightly stronger taste.

Red split lentils

Popular and easy to cook, these lentils are often used in vegetarian dishes.

TOFU

This is an unfermented soya bean curd that is available in firm and silken varieties to be used in all kinds of sweet and savoury dishes as an alternative to dairy produce.

Spices

The inclusion of spices in a recipe can literally transform a meal.

Cardamom
These pods are often used whole to add flavour to rice dishes.

Chilli powder
The dried seeds of chillies are ground to make a very hot and spicy powder.

Cinnamon
Cinnamon is available whole or ground. The sticks are used for flavour and are not eaten.

Cloves
Cloves are used in spice mixtures for sweet and savoury dishes.

Coriander seeds
These are the roasted, dried seeds of the plant.

Cumin
Available as whole, dark brown seeds and ground.

Fennel seeds
Small, light green seeds, similar in smell and taste to aniseed.

Fenugreek seeds
Fenugreek is used in many fish dishes and curries.

Ginger
Both fresh and ground ginger have a sharp, refreshing flavour. Fresh root ginger should be peeled before use.

Mustard seeds
Often used with vegetables and pulses, these have a nutty flavour.

Nutmeg
Whole or ground, nutmeg has a sweet, nutty flavour.

Peppercorns
Used in virtually all savoury cooking, pepper has the capacity to enhance other flavours.

Saffron
This expensive spice is used for its aroma and colour.

Turmeric
Turmeric is a bright yellow powder and is primarily used for its colouring properties.

Herbs

Beautiful fresh herbs from around the world are readily available. This herb checklist highlights both familiar and less well-known items.

Basil
Well-known for its affinity with tomatoes, basil has a spicy aroma that is a pungent mixture of cinnamon and anise.

Bay leaves
These are one of the oldest herbs used in cookery. When used fresh, they have a deliciously sweet flavour.

Chives
This herb has a very delicate oniony flavour.

Coriander
An intense, aromatic, sweet and spicy herb. The leaves can be used as a garnish.

Dill
A pungent, slightly sweet-tasting herb with anise overtones.

Marjoram
This is very similar to oregano, though more delicate in flavour.

Mint
A very versatile herb with a distinctive scent, mint is used both in sweet and savoury dishes.

Oregano
An aromatic and highly flavoured herb, oregano features strongly in Italian cooking.

Parsley
Both flat leaf and curly varieties have a slightly bitter flavour.

Rosemary
Rosemary, with its dark, needle-like leaves, has an intense flavour and should be used sparingly.

Sage
The aromatic oils in sage impart a distinct and powerful flavour.

Savory
With its peppery flavour, savory makes a good seasoning.

Tarragon
This has a sweet, aniseed flavour.

Thyme
A robust aromatic herb with a warm, earthy flavour.

Dry Goods

Building up a store cupboard of everyday items such as flours, grains and pasta will ensure that you can produce a speedy meal at short notice.

Barley
With its distinctive flavour and slightly chewy texture, barley is used in soups or as an alternative to rice in risottos.

Buckwheat
Nutty in texture, this tasty alternative to rice is actually a grass.

Bulgur wheat
This wholewheat grain is steam-dried and cracked before sale, so it only needs a brief soaking before use. Keep it cool and dry in the cupboard, and it will last for a few months.

Couscous
Also made from wheat, this grain is a staple in North Africa and is prepared in exactly the same way as bulgur.

Dried fruit
Rich in dietary fibre, vitamins and minerals, dried fruits are delicious in a wide selection of dishes including muesli and pies. Because of their intense sweetness, they can be used as a healthy alternative to sugar in cooking.

Flours
As well as the usual white refined flour, try experimenting with other types including wholemeal, buckwheat, soya, rice or rye for a more interesting, nutty flavour in your baking. Cornflour is often used as a thickening agent for sauces.

Millet
High in protein, millet is used extensively in Southeast Asia and is cooked in the same way as rice.

Nuts and seeds
Nuts and seeds such as almond, cashew, brazil, sunflower, pumpkin and linseed are a valuable source of protein, calcium and Omega 3 fatty acids. Bought in bulk for economy, they will keep in the freezer for several months.

Oats
Available as rolled (porridge), jumbo or oatmeal, this grain is an excellent source of complex carbohydrates, vitamins and minerals.

Pasta
While fresh pasta is generally preferred both for flavour and for speed of cooking, the dried product is a very valuable store-cupboard ingredient. Italian pasta and Oriental noodles are both useful.

Quinoa
Another good source of protein, quinoa is a soft grain from South America.

Rice
There are many different types of rice. Basmati is thought to have a superior flavour, fragrance and texture, and a mixture of basmati and wild rice (not a true rice, but the seeds of an aquatic grass) works well.

Sugars
Used sparingly, you can impart a distinctive flavour to your sweet dishes by adding dried sugars such as molasses, demerara, raw cane and icing sugar, or liquid varieties including blackstrap molasses, honey and natural maple syrup.

Wheat, barley and rye flakes
These can be used in savoury or sweet crumbles and biscuits to provide a variety of tastes and textures.

rice

ground turmeric

ground cumin

caraway se

egg noo

penne

pecan nuts

spaghetti

garam masala

dried chillies

bulgur wheat

cornflour

mixed spice

black peppercorns

Chinese five-spice powder

pine nuts

poppy seeds

chilli powder

ground coriander

sea salt

thyme

sugar

long grain rice

granulated sugar

nuts

Bottled and Canned Goods

The store cupboard should be the backbone of your vegetarian kitchen. Stock it sensibly, and you'll always have the wherewithal to make a tasty, satisfying meal.

Canned pulses

Chick-peas, cannellini beans, green lentils, haricot beans and red kidney beans survive the canning process well. Wash in cold running water and drain well before use.

Canned vegetables

Although fresh vegetables are best for most cooking, some canned products are very useful. Artichoke hearts have a mild sweet flavour and are great for adding to stir-fries, salads, risottos or pizzas. Pimientos are canned whole red peppers, seeded and peeled. Canned tomatoes are an essential ingredient to have in the pantry. Additional useful items to include are sweetcorn and water chestnuts.

Mustard

Wholegrain or Dijon mustards are widely used both in cooking and in salad dressings.

Oils

Groundnut or sunflower oils are bland and will not mask or overpower delicate flavours. They are ideal for deep frying. Fiery chilli oil will liven up vegetable stir-fries, while tasty sesame oil will give them a rich nutty flavour. A good olive oil will suit most purposes, except deep frying, and extra-virgin olive oil, being more expensive, is best kept for salads.

Olives

Green or black olives now come in a variety of marinades. Olive paste is useful for pasta sauces.

Passata

This thick sauce is made from sieved tomatoes. It is mainly used in Italian cookery.

Pesto

This classic Italian sauce combines fresh basil, pine nuts, Parmesan, garlic and olive oil and is useful for pasta or grilled or roasted vegetables.

Soy sauce/Shoyu

Soy sauce is a thin, salty black liquid made from fermented soya beans. Shoyu, or naturally brewed soy sauce, is fermented for far longer and so has less additives than soy sauce.

Stocks and flavourings

There are three kinds of vegetable stocks. Granules are ideal for light soups and risottos, stock cubes have a stronger flavour suited to hearty soups, while vegetable extracts have a robust taste which is delicious in casseroles.

Sun-dried tomatoes

These deliciously sweet tomatoes, baked in the sun and dried, are sold in bags or in jars, steeped in olive oil.

Tahini paste

Made from ground sesame seeds, this paste is used in Middle Eastern cookery.

Tomato purée

This is a concentrated tomato paste which is sold in cans, jars or tubes. A version made from sun-dried tomatoes is now available.

Vinegars

White or red wine and sherry vinegars are ideal for salad dressings. Balsamic has a very distinctive sweet/sour flavour which can be used in salad dressings or to liven up roasted vegetables and cooked grains.

tahini paste

chopped tomatoes

chick-peas

tomato purée

syrup

red wine

chilli sauce

herb vinegar

sweetcorn

white wine
vinegar

chilli oil

black olive paste

pimientos

soy sauce

black bean
sauce

dney beans

lentils

plum tomatoes

chillies in oil

olive
oil

mustard

honey

tahini paste

ssata

groundnut oil

red-wine
vinegar

salad dressing

ghee

black olives

balsamic vinegar

SOUPS

Wild Mushroom Soup

Wild mushrooms are expensive, but dried porcini have an intense flavour, so only a small quantity is needed.

INGREDIENTS

Serves 4

25 g/1 oz/2 cups dried porcini mushrooms
30 ml/2 tbsp olive oil
15 g/½ oz/1 tbsp butter
2 leeks, thinly sliced
2 shallots, roughly chopped
1 garlic clove, roughly chopped
225 g/8 oz fresh wild mushrooms
about 1.2 litres/2 pints/5 cups vegetable
    stock
2.5 ml/½ tsp dried thyme
150 ml/¼ pint/⅔ cup double cream
salt and freshly ground black pepper
sprigs of fresh thyme, to garnish

1 Put the dried porcini in a bowl, add 250 ml/8 fl oz/1 cup warm water and leave to soak for 20–30 minutes. Lift out of the liquid and squeeze over the bowl to remove as much of the soaking liquid as possible. Strain all the liquid and reserve to use later. Finely chop the porcini.

2 Heat the oil and butter in a large saucepan until foaming. Add the sliced leeks, chopped shallots and garlic and cook gently for about 5 minutes, stirring frequently, until softened but not coloured.

3 Chop or slice the fresh mushrooms and add to the pan. Stir over a medium heat for a few minutes until they begin to soften. Pour in the stock and bring to the boil. Add the porcini, soaking liquid, dried thyme and salt and pepper. Lower the heat, half cover the pan and simmer gently for 30 minutes, stirring occasionally.

4 Pour about three-quarters of the soup into a blender or food processor and process until smooth. Return the processed soup to the soup remaining in the pan, stir in the cream and heat through. Check the consistency and add more stock if necessary. Season with salt and pepper. Serve hot, garnished with thyme sprigs.

COOK'S TIP

Porcini are ceps. Italian cooks would make this soup with a combination of fresh and dried ceps, but if fresh ceps are difficult to obtain, you can use other wild mushrooms such as chanterelles.

Tomato and Fresh Basil Soup

A pungent soup for late summer when fresh tomatoes are at their most flavoursome.

Serves 4–6

15 ml/1 tbsp olive oil
25 g/1 oz/2 tbsp butter
1 medium onion, finely chopped
900 g/2 1b ripe Italian plum tomatoes,
    roughly chopped
1 garlic clove, roughly chopped
about 750 ml/1¼ pints/3 cups vegetable
    stock
120 ml/4 fl oz/½ cup dry white wine
30 ml/2 tbsp sun-dried tomato paste
30 ml/2 tbsp shredded fresh basil
150 ml/¼ pint/⅔ cup double cream
salt and freshly ground black pepper
whole basil leaves, to garnish

1 Heat the oil and butter in a large saucepan until foaming. Add the onion and cook gently for about 5 minutes, stirring, until the onion is softened but not brown.

2 Stir in the chopped tomatoes and garlic, then add the stock, white wine and sun-dried tomato paste, with salt and pepper to taste. Bring to the boil, then lower the heat, half cover the pan and simmer gently for 20 minutes, stirring occasionally to stop the tomatoes sticking to the base of the pan.

3 Process the soup with the shredded basil in a blender or food processor, then press through a sieve into a clean pan.

4 Add the double cream and heat through, stirring. Do not allow the soup to approach boiling point. Check the consistency and add more stock if necessary and then season with salt and pepper. Pour into heated bowls and garnish with basil. Serve at once.

Cream of Courgette Soup

The beauty of this soup is its delicate colour, rich and creamy texture and subtle taste. If you prefer a more pronounced cheese flavour, use Gorgonzola instead of dolcelatte.

INGREDIENTS

Serves 4–6

30 ml/2 tbsp olive oil

15 g/½ oz/1 tbsp butter

1 medium onion, roughly chopped

900 g/2 lb courgettes, trimmed and sliced

5 ml/1 tsp dried oregano

about 600 ml/1 pint/2½ cups
   vegetable stock

115 g/4 oz dolcelatte cheese, rind
   removed, diced

300 ml/½ pint/1¼ cups single cream

salt and freshly ground black pepper

fresh oregano, extra dolcelatte and cream,
   to garnish

2 Add the courgettes and oregano with salt and pepper to taste. Cook over a medium heat for 10 minutes, stirring frequently. Pour in the stock and bring to the boil, stirring.

1 Heat the oil and butter in a large saucepan until foaming. Add the onion and cook gently for about 5 minutes, stirring frequently, until softened but not brown.

COOK'S TIP

To save time, trim off and discard the ends of the courgettes, cut them into thirds, then chop in a food processor fitted with a metal blade.

3 Lower the heat, half cover the pan and simmer gently, stirring occasionally, for about 30 minutes. Stir in the diced dolcelatte until melted.

4 Process the soup in a blender or food processor until smooth, then press through a sieve into a clean pan.

5 Add two-thirds of the cream and stir over a low heat until hot, but not boiling. Add more stock or water if the soup is too thick. Season with salt and pepper. Pour into heated bowls. Swirl in the remaining cream. Serve, garnished with oregano, extra cheese, cream and pepper.

Garlic, Chick-pea and Spinach Soup

This delicious, thick and creamy soup is richly flavoured and makes a great one-pot meal.

Serves 4

30 ml/2 tbsp olive oil
4 garlic cloves, crushed
1 onion, roughly chopped
10 ml/2 tsp ground cumin
10 ml/2 tsp ground coriander
1.2 litres/2 pints/5 cups vegetable stock
350 g/12 oz potatoes, peeled and
    finely chopped
425 g/15 oz can chick-peas, drained
15 ml/1 tbsp cornflour
150 ml/¼ pint/⅔ cup double cream
30 ml/2 tbsp light tahini (sesame
    seed paste)
200 g/7 oz spinach, shredded
cayenne pepper
salt and freshly ground black pepper

1 Heat the oil in a large saucepan and cook the garlic and onion for 5 minutes, or until they are softened and golden brown.

2 Stir in the cumin and coriander and cook for a further minute.

3 Pour in the stock and add the chopped potatoes to the pan. Bring to the boil and simmer for 10 minutes. Add the chick-peas and simmer for a further 5 minutes, or until the potatoes and chick-peas are just tender.

4 Blend together the cornflour, cream, tahini and plenty of seasoning. Stir into the soup with the spinach. Bring to the boil, stirring, and simmer for a further 2 minutes. Season with cayenne pepper, salt and black pepper. Serve immediately, sprinkled with a little cayenne pepper.

Classic French Onion Soup

When French onion soup is made slowly and carefully, the onions almost caramelize to a deep mahogany colour. It has a superb flavour and is a perfect winter supper dish.

INGREDIENTS

Serves 4

4 large onions

30 ml/2 tbsp sunflower or olive oil, or
  15ml/1 tbsp of each

25 g/1 oz/2 tbsp butter

900 ml/1½ pints/3¾ cups vegetable stock

4 slices French bread

40–50 g/1½–2 oz Gruyère or Cheddar
  cheese, grated

salt and freshly ground black pepper

1 Peel and quarter the onions and slice or chop them into 5 mm/¼ in pieces. Heat the oil and butter in a deep saucepan, preferably with a medium-size base so that the onions form a thick layer.

2 Fry the onions briskly for a few minutes, stirring constantly.

3 Reduce the heat and cook gently for 45–60 minutes. At first, the onions need to be stirred only occasionally but as they begin to colour, stir frequently. The colour of the onions gradually turns golden and then more rapidly to brown, so take care to stir constantly at this stage so that they do not burn on the base.

4 When the onions are a rich mahogany brown, add the vegetable stock and a little seasoning. Simmer, partially covered, for 30 minutes, then season with salt and pepper.

5 Preheat the grill and toast the French bread. Spoon the soup into four ovenproof serving dishes and place a piece of bread in each. Sprinkle with the cheese and grill for a few minutes until golden. Season with plenty of freshly ground black pepper.

White Bean Soup

A thick purée of cooked dried beans is at the heart of this substantial country soup from Tuscany. It makes a warming lunch or supper dish.

INGREDIENTS

Serves 6

350 g/12 oz/1½ cups dried cannellini or other white beans

1 bay leaf

75 ml/5 tbsp olive oil

1 medium onion, finely chopped

1 carrot, finely chopped

1 stick celery, finely chopped

3 medium tomatoes, peeled and finely chopped

2 cloves garlic, finely chopped

5 ml/1 tsp fresh thyme leaves or 2.5 ml/ ½ tsp dried thyme

750 ml/1¼ pints/3 cups boiling water

salt and freshly ground black pepper

olive oil, to serve

1 Pick over the beans carefully, discarding any stones or other particles. Rinse thoroughly in cold water to ensure that they are clean. Soak in a large bowl of cold water overnight. Drain the beans and place them in a large saucepan of water, bring to the boil and cook for 20 minutes. Drain. Return the beans to the pan, cover with cold water and bring to the boil again. Add the bay leaf and cook until the beans are tender for approximately 1–2 hours. Drain again. Remove the bay leaf.

2 Purée about three-quarters of the beans in a food processor, or pass through a food mill, adding a little water if necessary, to create a smooth paste.

3 Heat the oil in a large saucepan. Stir in the onion and cook until it softens. Add the carrot and celery, and cook for 5 minutes more.

4 Stir in the tomatoes, garlic and thyme. Cook for 6–8 minutes more, stirring often.

5 Pour in the boiling water. Stir in the beans and the bean purée. Season with salt and pepper. Simmer for 10–15 minutes. Serve in individual soup bowls, sprinkled with a little olive oil.

COOK'S TIP

Other types of canned cooked beans, such as cannellini or borlotti, may be substituted in this recipe. Simply drain the beans and omit Step 1.

Asparagus Soup

Home-made asparagus soup has a delicate flavour, quite unlike that from a can. This soup is best made with young asparagus, which are tender and blend well. Serve it with wafer-thin slices of bread.

Serves 4

450 g/1 lb young asparagus

40 g/1½ oz/3 tbsp butter

6 shallots, sliced

15 g/½ oz/1 tbsp plain flour

600 ml/1 pint/2½ cups vegetable stock or
    water

15 ml/1 tbsp lemon juice

250 ml/8 fl oz/1 cup milk

120 ml/4 fl oz/½ cup single cream

10 ml/2 tsp chopped fresh chervil

salt and freshly ground black pepper

1 Cut 4 cm/1½ in off the tops of half the asparagus and set aside for a garnish. Slice the remaining asparagus.

2 Melt 25 g/1 oz/2 tbsp of the butter in a large saucepan and fry the sliced shallots for 2–3 minutes until soft.

3 Add the asparagus and fry over a low heat for about 1 minute.

4 Stir in the flour and cook for 1 minute. Stir in the stock or water and lemon juice and season with salt and pepper. Bring to the boil, half cover the pan, then simmer for 15–20 minutes, until the asparagus is very tender.

5 Cool slightly and then process the soup in a food processor or blender until smooth. Press the puréed asparagus through a sieve into a clean saucepan. Add the milk by pouring and stirring it through the sieve with the asparagus so as to extract the maximum amount of asparagus purée.

6 Melt the remaining butter and fry the reserved asparagus tips gently for 3–4 minutes to soften.

7 Heat the soup gently for 3–4 minutes. Stir in the cream and the asparagus tips. Continue to heat gently and serve sprinkled with chopped fresh chervil.

Fresh Tomato, Lentil and Onion Soup

*This delicious wholesome soup is
ideal served with thick slices of
wholemeal or granary bread.*

INGREDIENTS

Serves 4–6

10 ml/2 tsp sunflower oil

1 large onion, chopped

2 sticks celery, chopped

175 g/6 oz/¾ cup split red lentils

2 large tomatoes, skinned and roughly
   chopped

900 ml/1½ pints/3¾ cups vegetable stock

10 ml/2 tsp dried herbes de Provence

salt and freshly ground black pepper

chopped parsley, to garnish

1 Heat the oil in a large
saucepan. Add the onion and
celery and cook for 5 minutes,
stirring occasionally. Add the
lentils and cook for 1 minute.

2 Stir in the tomatoes, stock,
dried herbs, salt and pepper.
Cover, bring to the boil and
simmer for about 20 minutes,
stirring occasionally.

3 When the lentils are cooked
and tender, set the soup aside
to cool slightly.

4 Purée in a blender or food
processor until smooth.
Season with salt and pepper,
return to the saucepan and reheat
gently until piping hot. Ladle into
soup bowls to serve and garnish
each with chopped parsley.

Minestrone with Pesto

*Minestrone is a thick, mixed
vegetable soup using almost any
combination of seasonal vegetables.
Short pasta or rice may also be
added. This version includes
pesto sauce.*

INGREDIENTS

Serves 6

45 ml/3 tbsp olive oil

1 large onion, finely chopped

1 leek, sliced

2 carrots, finely chopped

1 stick celery, finely chopped

2 cloves garlic, finely chopped

2 potatoes, peeled and cut into small dice

1.5 litres/2½ pints/6¼ cups hot vegetable
stock or water, or a combination of
both

1 bay leaf

1 sprig of fresh thyme, or 1.5 ml/¼ tsp
dried thyme

115 g/4 oz/¾ cup peas, fresh or frozen

2–3 courgettes, finely chopped

3 medium tomatoes, peeled and finely
chopped

425 g/15 oz/2 cups cooked or canned
beans, such as cannellini

45 ml/3 tbsp pesto sauce

salt and freshly ground black pepper

freshly grated Parmesan cheese, to serve

1 Heat the oil in a saucepan. Stir
in the onion and leek, and cook
for 5–6 minutes. Add the carrots,
celery and garlic, and cook over
moderate heat for 5 minutes. Add
the potatoes and cook for 2–3
minutes more.

2 Pour in the hot stock or water,
and stir well. Add the herbs
and season with salt and pepper.
Bring to the boil, reduce the heat
and cook for 10–12 minutes.

3 Stir in the peas, if fresh, and the
courgettes. Simmer for 5
minutes more. Add the frozen peas,
if using, and the tomatoes. Cover
the pan and boil for 5–8 minutes.

4 About 10 minutes before
serving, uncover and stir in the
beans. Simmer for 10 minutes. Stir
in the pesto sauce. Simmer for
another 5 minutes. Remove from
heat and allow to stand for a few
minutes. Serve with the grated
Parmesan cheese.

Pumpkin Soup

*This beautifully flavoured, golden-
coloured soup would be perfect for
an autumn dinner.*

INGREDIENTS

Serves 4

450 g/1 lb piece of peeled pumpkin

50 g/2 oz/¼ cup butter

1 medium onion, finely chopped

750 ml/1¼ pints/3 cups vegetable stock
or water

475 ml/16 fl oz/2 cups milk

pinch of grated nutmeg

40 g/1½ oz/7 tbsp spaghetti, broken into
small pieces

90 ml/6 tbsp freshly grated Parmesan
cheese

salt and freshly ground black pepper

1 Chop the piece of pumpkin
into 2.5 cm/1 in cubes.

2 Heat the butter in a saucepan.
Add the onion and cook over
moderate heat until it softens, 6–8
minutes. Stir in the pumpkin
pieces and cook for about 2–3
minutes more.

3 Add the stock or water and
cook until the pumpkin is soft,
about 15 minutes. Remove from
the heat.

4 Process the soup in a blender
or food processor. Return it to
the pan. Stir in the milk and
nutmeg. Season with salt and
pepper. Bring the soup back to
the boil.

5 Stir the broken spaghetti into
the soup. Cook until the pasta
is done. Stir in the Parmesan,
sprinkle with nutmeg and serve
at once.

Split Pea and Courgette Soup

Rich and satisfying, this tasty and nutritious soup will warm a chilly winter's day.

INGREDIENTS

Serves 4

175 g/6 oz/1⅞ cups yellow split peas

1 medium onion, finely chopped

5 ml/1 tsp sunflower oil

2 medium courgettes, finely diced

900 ml/1½ pints/3¾ cups vegetable stock

2.5 ml/½ tsp ground turmeric

salt and freshly ground black pepper

crusty bread, to serve

3 Add the remaining courgettes to the pan. Cook for 2–3 minutes. Add the stock, turmeric and split peas and bring to the boil. Reduce the heat, cover and simmer for 30–40 minutes. Season.

4 When the soup is almost ready, bring a large saucepan of water to the boil, add the reserved diced courgettes and cook for 1 minute. Drain and add to the soup. Serve hot with warm crusty bread.

1 Place the split peas in a bowl, cover with cold water and leave to soak for several hours or overnight. Drain, rinse in cold water and drain again.

2 Cook the onion in the oil in a covered pan, shaking occasionally, until soft. Reserve a handful of diced courgettes to use later.

COOK'S TIP

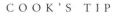

For a quicker alternative, use red split lentils for this soup – they need no presoaking and cook very quickly. Adjust the amount of stock, if necessary.

Carrot and Coriander Soup

Nearly all root vegetables make excellent soups as they purée well and have an earthy flavour, which complements the sharper flavours of herbs and spices. Carrots are particularly versatile, and this simple soup is elegant in both flavour and appearance.

INGREDIENTS

Serves 4–6

450 g/1 lb carrots, preferably young and
   tender
15 ml/1 tbsp sunflower oil
40 g/1½ oz/3 tbsp butter
1 onion, chopped
1 stick celery, plus 2–3 pale leafy
   celery tops
2 small potatoes, peeled
1 litre/1¾ pints/4 cups vegetable stock
10-15 ml/2-3 tsp ground coriander
15 ml/1 tbsp chopped fresh coriander
200 ml/7 fl oz/⅞ cup milk
salt and freshly ground black pepper

1 Trim and peel the carrots and cut into chunks. Heat the oil and 25 g/1 oz/2 tbsp butter in a large flameproof casserole or heavy-based saucepan and fry the onion over a gentle heat for 3–4 minutes, until slightly softened.

2 Slice the celery and chop the potatoes. Add them to the onion in the pan, cook for a few minutes and then add the carrots. Fry over a gentle heat for 3–4 minutes, stirring, and then cover.

3 Reduce the heat even further and sweat for about 10 minutes. Shake the pan or stir occasionally so the vegetables do not stick to the base.

4 Add the stock and bring to the boil. Half cover the pan and simmer for a further 8–10 minutes, until the carrots and potatoes are tender.

5 Remove 6–8 tiny celery leaves for garnish and finely chop the remaining celery tops (about 15 ml/1 tbsp once chopped). Melt the remaining butter in a small saucepan and fry the ground coriander for about 1 minute, stirring constantly.

6 Reduce the heat and add the chopped celery tops and fresh coriander and fry for about 1 minute. Set aside.

7 Process the soup in a food processor or blender and pour into a clean saucepan. Stir in the milk and coriander mixture. Season, heat gently, taste and adjust seasoning. Serve garnished with the reserved celery leaves.

C O O K ' S   T I P

For a more piquant flavour, add a little lemon juice just before serving.

Curried Celery Soup

An unusual combination of flavours, this warming soup is excellent served with warm wholemeal bread rolls or wholemeal pitta bread.

Serves 4–6

10 ml/2 tsp olive oil
1 onion, chopped
1 leek, washed and sliced
675 g/1½ lb celery, chopped
15 ml/1 tbsp medium or hot curry powder
225 g/8 oz unpeeled potatoes, washed and diced
900 ml/1½ pints/3¾ cups vegetable stock
1 bouquet garni
30 ml/2 tbsp chopped fresh mixed herbs
salt
celery seeds and leaves, to garni

2 Add the curry powder and cook for a further 2 minutes, stirring occasionally.

3 Add the potatoes, stock and bouquet garni, cover and bring to the boil. Simmer for 20 minutes, until the vegetables are tender.

4 Remove and discard the bouquet garni and set the soup aside to cool slightly.

5 Purée in a blender or food processor until smooth.

6 Add the mixed herbs, season to taste and process briefly. Return to the saucepan and reheat gently until piping hot. Ladle into soup bowls and garnish each with a sprinkling of celery seeds and some celery leaves.

1 Heat the oil in a large saucepan. Add the onion, leek and celery, cover and cook gently for about 10 minutes, stirring occasionally.

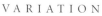

VARIATION

For a tasty change, use celeriac and sweet potatoes in place of the celery and standard potatoes.

Fresh Pea Soup

This soup is known in France as Potage Saint-Germain, a name which comes from a suburb of Paris where peas used to be cultivated in market gardens. If fresh peas are not available, use frozen peas, but thaw and rinse them before use.

INGREDIENTS

Serves 2–3

25 g/1 oz/2 tbsp butter

2 or 3 shallots, finely chopped

400 g/14 oz/3 cups shelled fresh peas
    (from about 1.3 kg/3 lb garden peas) or
    thawed frozen peas

45-60 ml/3–4 tbsp whipping cream
    (optional)

salt and freshly ground black pepper

croûtons, to garnish

1 Melt the butter in a heavy saucepan or flameproof casserole. Add the shallots and cook for about 3 minutes, stirring occasionally.

2 Add 500 ml/16 fl oz/2 cups water and the peas, and season with salt and pepper.

3 Cover and simmer for 12 minutes for young or frozen peas and up to 18 minutes for large or older peas, stirring occasionally.

4 When the peas are tender, ladle them into a food processor or blender with a little of the cooking liquid and process until smooth.

5 Strain the soup into the saucepan or casserole, stir in the cream, if using, and heat through without boiling. Season with salt and pepper and serve hot garnished with croûtons.

Pea, Leek and Broccoli Soup

A delicious and nutritious soup, ideal for warming those chilly winter evenings.

INGREDIENTS

Serves 4–6

1 onion, chopped

225 g/8 oz/2 cups leeks (trimmed weight), sliced

225 g/8 oz unpeeled potatoes, diced

900 ml/1½ pints/3¾ cups vegetable stock

1 bay leaf

225 g/8 oz broccoli florets

175 g/6 oz/1½ cups frozen peas

30–45 ml/2–3 tbsp chopped fresh parsley

salt and freshly ground black pepper

parsley leaves, to garnish

1 Put the onion, leeks, potatoes, stock and bay leaf in a large saucepan and mix together. Cover, bring to the boil and simmer for 10 minutes, stirring.

2 Add the broccoli and peas, cover, return to the boil and simmer for a further 10 minutes, stirring occasionally.

3 Set aside to cool slightly and remove and discard the bay leaf. Purée in a blender or food processor until smooth.

4 Add the parsley, season with salt and pepper and process briefly. Return to the saucepan and reheat gently until piping hot. Ladle into soup bowls and garnish with parsley leaves.

Gazpacho

This cold soup is popular all over Spain, where there are hundreds of variations. It uses tomatoes, tomato juice, green pepper and garlic, and is served with a selection of garnishes.

INGREDIENTS

Serves 4

1.5 kg/3–3½ lb ripe tomatoes

1 green pepper, seeded and
   roughly chopped

2 garlic cloves, crushed

2 slices white bread, crusts removed

60 ml/4 tbsp olive oil

60 ml/4 tbsp tarragon wine vinegar

150 ml/¼ pint/⅔ cup tomato juice

good pinch of sugar

salt and freshly ground black pepper

ice cubes, to serve

For the garnishes

30 ml/2 tbsp sunflower oil

2–3 slices white bread, diced

1 small cucumber, peeled and finely diced

1 small onion, finely chopped

1 red pepper, seeded and finely diced

1 green pepper, seeded and finely diced

2 hard-boiled eggs, chopped

1 Skin and quarter the tomatoes, then remove the cores.

2 Place the pepper in a food processor and process for a few seconds. Add the tomatoes, garlic, bread, olive oil and vinegar and process again. Add the tomato juice, sugar, salt and pepper and process.

3 The mixture should be thick but not too stodgy. Continue processing until it is the right consistency. Press the liquid through a sieve into a bowl and chill for at least 2 hours but no more than 12 hours, otherwise the texture will deteriorate.

4 To prepare the bread cubes to use as a garnish, heat the oil in a frying pan and fry them over a moderate heat for 4–5 minutes, until golden brown. Drain well on kitchen paper.

5 Place each garnish in a separate small dish, or alternatively arrange them in rows on a large plate.

6 Just before serving, stir a few ice cubes into the soup and then spoon into serving bowls. Serve with the garnishes.

Cold Leek and Potato Soup

Serve this flavourful soup with a dollop of crème fraîche or soured cream to add richness to this warming broth on cold winter evenings. Sprinkle with a few snipped fresh chives.

INGREDIENTS

Serves 6–8

450 g/1 lb potatoes, peeled and cubed
1.5 litres/2½ pints/6¼ cups vegetable stock
4 medium leeks, trimmed
150 ml/¼ pint/⅔ cup crème fraîche or
   soured cream
salt and freshly ground black pepper
45 ml/3 tbsp snipped fresh chives,
   to garnish

1 Put the potatoes and stock in a saucepan or flameproof casserole and bring to the boil. Reduce the heat and simmer for 15–20 minutes.

2 Make a slit along the length of each leek and rinse well under cold running water. Slice thinly.

3 When the potatoes are barely tender, stir in the leeks. Season with salt and pepper and simmer for 10–15 minutes until the vegetables are soft, stirring occasionally. If the soup appears too thick, thin it down with a little more of the stock or water.

4 Purée the soup in a blender or food processor, in batches if necessary. If you would prefer a very smooth soup, pass it through a food mill or press through a coarse sieve. Stir in most of the cream, cool and then chill. To serve, ladle into chilled bowls and garnish with a swirl of cream and snipped chives.

VARIATION

To make a low-fat soup, use low-fat fromage frais instead of crème fraîche or soured cream, or simply thin the soup with a little skimmed milk.

STARTERS

Guacamole

This is quite a fiery version, although nowhere near as hot as you would be served in Mexico!

INGREDIENTS

Serves 4

2 ripe avocados, peeled and stoned

2 tomatoes, peeled, seeded and finely chopped

6 spring onions, finely chopped

1–2 fresh chillies, seeded and finely chopped

30 ml/2 tbsp fresh lime or lemon juice

15 ml/1 tbsp chopped fresh coriander

salt and freshly ground black pepper

coriander sprigs, to garnish

1 Put the avocado halves into a large bowl and mash them roughly with a large fork.

2 Add the remaining ingredients. Mix well and season with salt and pepper. Serve garnished with fresh coriander.

Butter Bean, Watercress and Herb Dip

This is a refreshing dip that is especially good served with fresh vegetable crudités and breadsticks.

Serves 4–6

225 g/8 oz/1 cup plain cottage cheese
400 g/14 oz can butter beans, rinsed
    and drained
1 bunch spring onions, chopped
50 g/2 oz watercress, chopped
60 ml/4 tbsp mayonnaise
45 ml/3 tbsp chopped fresh mixed herbs
salt and freshly ground black pepper
watercress sprigs, to garnish
vegetable crudités and breadsticks,
    to serve

1 Put the cottage cheese, butter beans, spring onions, watercress, mayonnaise and herbs in a blender or food processor and blend until fairly smooth.

2 Season with salt and pepper and spoon the mixture into a dish.

3 Cover and chill for several hours before serving.

4 Transfer to a serving dish (or individual dishes) and garnish with watercress sprigs. Serve with vegetable crudités and breadsticks.

COOK'S TIP

Try using other canned beans such as cannellini beans or chickpeas in place of the butter beans.

Saffron Dip

Serve this mild dip with fresh vegetable crudités – it is particularly good with florets of cauliflower.

Serves 4

small pinch of saffron strands
200 g/7 oz fromage frais
10 fresh chives
10 fresh basil leaves
salt and freshly ground black pepper
vegetable crudités, to serve

1 Pour 15 ml/1 tbsp boiling water into a small heatproof bowl and add the saffron strands. Leave to infuse for about 3–4 minutes, stirring occasionally.

2 Beat the fromage frais until smooth, then stir in the infused saffron liquid.

3 Use a pair of scissors to snip the chives into the dip. Tear the basil leaves into small pieces and stir them in.

4 Season with salt and pepper. Serve immediately with vegetable crudités.

VARIATION

Leave out the saffron and add a squeeze of lemon or lime juice instead. Alternatively, substitute the saffron strands with ready-ground saffron powder.

Spiced Carrot Dip

This is a delicious dip with a sweet and spicy flavour. Serve wheat crackers or fiery tortilla chips as accompaniments for dipping.

INGREDIENTS

Serves 4

1 onion

3 carrots, plus extra to garnish

grated rind and juice of 2 oranges

15 ml/1 tbsp hot curry paste

150 ml/¼ pint/⅔ cup natural yogurt

handful of fresh basil leaves

15–30 ml/1–2 tbsp fresh lemon juice, to taste

red Tabasco sauce, to taste

salt and freshly ground black pepper

3 Stir in the yogurt, then tear the basil leaves roughly into small pieces and stir them into the carrot mixture.

4 Add the lemon juice and Tabasco and season with salt and pepper. Serve within a few hours at room temperature. Garnish with grated carrot.

1 Finely chop the onion. Peel and grate the carrots. Place the onion, carrots, orange rind and juice, and curry paste in a small saucepan. Bring to the boil, cover and simmer gently for 10 minutes, until tender.

2 Process the mixture in a blender or food processor until smooth. Leave to cool completely.

Aubergine Dip with Crispy Bread

This delectable Middle Eastern dish is flavoured with tahini (sesame seed paste), which gives it a subtle hint of spice.

INGREDIENTS

Serves 6

2 small aubergines

1 garlic clove, crushed

60 ml/4 tbsp tahini (sesame seed paste)

25 g/1 oz/¼ cup ground almonds

juice of ½ lemon

2.5 ml/½ tsp ground cumin

30 ml/2 tbsp fresh mint leaves

30 ml/2 tbsp olive oil

salt and freshly ground black pepper

Lebanese flatbread

4 pitta breads

45 ml/3 tbsp toasted sesame seeds

45 ml/3 tbsp fresh thyme leaves, chopped

45 ml/3 tbsp poppy seeds

150 ml/¼ pint/⅔ cup olive oil

3 Grill the aubergines, turning them frequently, until the skin is blackened and blistered. Remove the skin, chop the flesh roughly and leave to drain in a colander. Wait for 30 minutes, then squeeze out as much liquid from the aubergines as possible.

4 Place the flesh in a blender or food processor. Add the garlic, tahini, almonds, lemon juice and cumin. Season, and process to a smooth paste. Chop half the mint and stir in.

5 Spoon into a bowl, scatter the remaining mint leaves on top and drizzle with olive oil. Serve with the Lebanese flatbread.

1 Start by making the Lebanese flatbread. Split the pitta breads through the middle and carefully open them out. Mix the sesame seeds, chopped thyme and poppy seeds in a mortar. Crush them lightly with a pestle to release the flavour.

2 Stir in the olive oil. Spread the mixture lightly over the cut sides of the pitta bread. Grill until golden brown and crisp. When completely cool, break into pieces and set aside.

Chick-pea Falafel with Coriander Dip

*Little balls of spicy chick-pea purée,
deep-fried until crisp, are served
with a zesty coriander-flavoured
mayonnaise.*

INGREDIENTS

Serves 4

400 g/14 oz can chick-peas, drained

6 spring onions, finely chopped

1 egg

2.5 ml/½ tsp ground turmeric

1 garlic clove, crushed

5 ml/1 tsp ground cumin

60 ml/4 tbsp chopped fresh coriander

oil for deep-frying

1 small fresh red chilli, seeded and
    finely chopped

45 ml/3 tbsp mayonnaise

salt and freshly ground black pepper

sprig of fresh coriander, to garnish

1 Put the chick-peas into a food
processor or blender. Add the
spring onions and process to a
smooth purée. Add the egg,
ground turmeric, garlic, cumin
and about 15 ml/1 tbsp of the
chopped coriander. Process
briefly to mix, then season with
salt and pepper.

2 Working with clean, wet hands,
shape the chick-pea mixture
into about 16 small balls.

3 Heat the oil for deep-frying to
180°C/350°F or until a cube of
bread, when added to the oil,
browns in 30–45 seconds. Deep-
fry the falafel in batches for 2–3
minutes or until golden. Drain the
falafel on kitchen paper. Place in a
serving bowl and keep warm.

4 Stir the remaining chopped
coriander and the chilli into
the mayonnaise. Garnish with the
coriander sprig and serve
alongside the falafel.

Hummus with Pan-fried Courgettes

Pan-fried courgettes are perfect for dipping into home-made hummus, served with pitta bread and olives.

INGREDIENTS

Serves 4

225 g/8 oz can chick-peas
2 garlic cloves, coarsely crushed
90 ml/6 tbsp lemon juice
60 ml/4 tbsp tahini (sesame seed paste)
75 ml/5 tbsp olive oil, plus extra to serve
5 ml/1 tsp ground cumin
450 g/1 lb small courgettes
salt and freshly ground black pepper
paprika and black olives, to garnish
pitta bread, to serve

2 Mix the garlic, lemon juice and tahini together and add to the blender or food processor. Process until smooth. With the machine running, gradually add 45 ml/3 tbsp of the olive oil through the feeder tube or lid.

5 Heat the remaining oil in a large frying pan. Season the courgettes with salt and pepper and fry them for 2–3 minutes on each side, until just tender.

1 Drain the chick-peas, reserving the liquid from the can, and put them into a blender or food processor. Blend to a smooth paste, adding a small amount of the reserved liquid, if necessary.

3 Add the cumin. Season with salt and pepper. Process to mix. Scrape the hummus into a bowl. Cover and chill until required.

6 Divide the courgettes among four individual plates. Spoon a portion of hummus on to each plate and sprinkle with paprika. Add two or three pieces of sliced pitta bread and serve with olives.

4 Remove the ends from the courgettes. Slice the courgettes lengthways into even-size pieces.

VARIATION

For a stronger nutty flavour, substitute the tahini paste with smooth peanut butter. This is also delicious served with pan-fried or grilled aubergine slices or red peppers.

Marinated Vegetable Antipasto

This colourful selection of fresh vegetables and herbs makes a great starter when served with fresh crusty bread.

INGREDIENTS

Serves 4

For the peppers

3 red peppers

3 yellow peppers

4 garlic cloves, sliced

handful of fresh basil

120 ml/4 fl oz/½ cup olive oil

salt and freshly ground black pepper

For the mushrooms

450 g/1 lb open cap mushrooms, thickly sliced

60 ml/4 tbsp olive oil

1 large garlic clove, crushed

15 ml/1 tbsp chopped fresh rosemary

250 ml/8 fl oz/1 cup dry white wine

fresh rosemary sprigs, to garnish

For the olives

1 dried red chilli, crushed

grated rind of 1 lemon

120 ml/4 fl oz/½ cup olive oil

225 g/8 oz/1⅓ cups Italian black olives

30 ml/2 tbsp chopped fresh flat leaf parsley

basil leaves, to garnish

1 lemon wedge, to serve

1 Place the peppers under a hot grill. Cook until they are black and blistered all over. Remove from the heat and place in a large plastic bag to cool.

2 When the peppers are cool, remove their skins, halve the flesh and remove the seeds. Cut into strips lengthways and place them in a bowl with the sliced garlic and basil leaves. Season and then cover with oil and marinate for 3–4 hours, tossing occasionally. Garnish with basil leaves.

3 Place the mushrooms in a large bowl. Heat the oil in a pan and add the garlic, rosemary and wine. Bring to the boil, then simmer for 3 minutes. Season. Pour over the mushrooms.

4 Mix well and leave to cool, stirring occasionally. Cover and marinate overnight. Serve at room temperature, garnished with rosemary sprigs.

5 Place the chilli and lemon rind in a small pan with the oil. Heat gently for about 3 minutes. Add the olives and heat for 1 minute more. Tip the olive mixture into a bowl and leave to cool. Marinate overnight. Before serving, sprinkle with parsley and garnish with basil leaves. Serve with the lemon wedge.

Spicy Potato Wedges with Chilli Dip

The spicy crust on these potato wedges makes them irresistible, especially when served with a zesty chilli dip.

INGREDIENTS

Serves 2

2 baking potatoes, about 225 g/8 oz each

30 ml/2 tbsp olive oil

2 garlic cloves, crushed

5 ml/1 tsp ground allspice

5 ml/1 tsp ground coriander

15 ml/1 tbsp paprika

salt and freshly ground black pepper

For the dip

15 ml/1 tbsp olive oil

1 small onion, finely chopped

1 garlic clove, crushed

200 g/7 oz can chopped tomatoes

1 fresh red chilli, seeded and
   finely chopped

15 ml/1 tbsp balsamic vinegar

15 ml/1 tbsp chopped fresh coriander,
   plus extra to garnish

1 Preheat the oven to 200°C/400°F/Gas 6. Wash the potatoes, cut in half, then into 8 wedges.

2 Place the potato wedges in a saucepan of cold water. Bring to the boil, then lower the heat and simmer gently for 10 minutes, or until the potatoes have softened slightly. Drain well and pat dry on kitchen paper.

3 Mix the oil, garlic, allspice, coriander and paprika in a roasting tin. Season with salt and pepper. Add the potatoes and shake to coat thoroughly. Roast for 20 minutes, turning occasionally.

4 Meanwhile, make the chilli dip. Heat the oil in a saucepan, add the onion and garlic and cook for 5–10 minutes until soft and golden. Add the tomatoes with their juice and stir in the chilli and vinegar.

5 Cook gently for 10 minutes, until the mixture has reduced and thickened. Season with salt and pepper. Stir in the fresh coriander and serve hot, with the potato wedges. Garnish with salt, freshly ground black pepper and fresh coriander.

Crispy Spring Rolls with Sweet Chilli Dip

Dainty miniature spring rolls make delicious appetizers or perfect party finger food.

INGREDIENTS

Makes 20–24

25 g/1 oz rice vermicelli noodles

peanut oil

5 ml/1 tsp fresh root ginger, finely grated

2 spring onions, finely shredded

50 g/2 oz carrot, finely shredded

50 g/2 oz mangetouts, shredded

25 g/1 oz young spinach leaves

50 g/2 oz fresh beansprouts

15 ml/1 tbsp fresh mint, finely chopped

15 ml/1 tbsp fresh coriander, finely chopped

30 ml/2 tbsp light soy sauce

20–24 spring roll wrappers, each 13 cm/ 5 in square

1 egg white, lightly beaten

For the dipping sauce

60 ml/4 tbsp sugar

50 ml/2 fl oz/¼ cup rice vinegar

2 fresh red chillies, seeded and finely chopped

1 First make the dipping sauce. Place the sugar and vinegar in a small saucepan with 30 ml/2 tbsp water. Heat gently, stirring until the sugar dissolves, then boil rapidly until it forms a light syrup. Stir in the chillies and leave to cool thoroughly.

2 Soak the noodles according to the package instructions. Rinse and drain well. Using scissors, snip the noodles into short lengths.

3 Heat a wok until hot. Add 15 ml/1 tbsp oil. Add the ginger and spring onions and stir-fry for 15 seconds. Add the carrot and mangetouts and stir-fry for 2–3 minutes. Add the spinach, beansprouts, mint, coriander, soy sauce and noodles and stir-fry for another minute. Set aside to cool.

4 Place a spring roll wrapper on the work surface. Put a spoonful of filling in the middle. Fold to encase the filling.

5 Fold in each side, then roll up tightly. Brush the end with beaten egg white to seal. Repeat until all the filling has been used.

6 Half-fill a wok with oil and heat to 180°C/350°F. Deep-fry the spring rolls in batches for 3–4 minutes, until golden and crisp. Drain on kitchen paper. Serve hot, with the sweet chilli dipping sauce.

COOK'S TIP

You can cook the spring rolls 2–3 hours in advance, then all you have to do is reheat them on a foil-lined baking sheet at 200°C/400°F/Gas 6 for about 10 minutes until they are ready to eat.

Potted Stilton with Herbs and Melba Toast

This starter is a great time saver, as the potted Stilton can be made the day before, and the Melba toast will keep in an airtight container for up to two days.

INGREDIENTS

Serves 8

225 g/8 oz/1 cup blue Stilton or other
 blue cheese
115 g/4 oz/½ cup cream cheese
15 ml/1 tbsp port
15 ml/1 tbsp chopped fresh parsley
15 ml/1 tbsp snipped fresh chives, plus
 extra to garnish
50 g/2 oz/½ cup finely chopped walnuts
salt and freshly ground black pepper

For the Melba toast
12 thin slices of white bread

1 Put the Stilton or blue cheese, cream cheese and port into a blender or food processor and process until smooth.

2 Stir in the remaining ingredients and then season with salt and pepper.

3 Spoon into individual ramekin dishes and level the tops. Cover with clear film and chill until firm. Sprinkle with snipped chives just before serving.

4 To make the Melba toast, preheat the oven to 180°C/350°F/Gas 4. Toast the bread on both sides.

5 While the toast is still hot, cut off the crusts and cut each slice horizontally in two. While the bread is still warm, place it in a single layer on baking trays and bake for 10–15 minutes, until golden brown and crisp. Continue with the remaining slices in the same way. Serve warm with the potted Stilton.

Mushroom and Bean Pâté

A light and tasty pâté, delicious served on wholemeal bread or toast.

INGREDIENTS

Serves 12

450 g/1 lb mushrooms, sliced
1 onion, chopped
2 garlic cloves, crushed
1 red pepper, seeded and diced
30 ml/2 tbsp vegetable stock
30 ml/2 tbsp dry white wine
400 g/14 oz can red kidney beans, rinsed
    and drained
1 egg, beaten
50 g/2 oz/1 cup fresh wholemeal
    breadcrumbs
15 ml/1 tbsp chopped fresh thyme
15 ml/1 tbsp chopped fresh rosemary
salt and freshly ground black pepper
lettuce and tomatoes, to garnish

1 Preheat the oven to 180°C/350°F/Gas 4. Lightly grease and line a non-stick 900 g/2 lb loaf tin. Put the mushrooms, onion, garlic, red pepper, stock and wine in a saucepan. Cover and cook for about 10 minutes, stirring occasionally.

2 Set aside to cool slightly, then purée the mixture with the kidney beans in a blender or food processor until smooth.

3 Transfer the mixture to a bowl, add the egg, breadcrumbs and herbs and mix thoroughly. Season with salt and pepper.

4 Spoon the mixture into the prepared tin and level the surface. Bake for 45–60 minutes, until lightly set and browned on top. Place on a wire rack and allow the pâté to cool completely in the tin. Once cool, cover and refrigerate for several hours. Turn out of the tin and serve in slices, garnished with lettuce and tomato.

Garlic Mushrooms with a Parsley Crust

These garlic mushrooms are perfect for dinner parties, or you could serve them in larger portions as a light supper dish with a green salad.

INGREDIENTS

Serves 4

350 g/12 oz large mushrooms, stems removed

3 garlic cloves, crushed

175 g/6 oz/¾ cup butter, softened

50 g/2 oz/1 cup fresh white breadcrumbs

50 g/2 oz/1 cup fresh parsley, chopped

1 egg, beaten

salt and cayenne pepper

8 cherry tomatoes, to garnish

1 Preheat the oven to 190°C/375°F/Gas 5. Arrange the mushrooms cup side uppermost on a baking tray. Mix together the garlic and butter in a small bowl and divide 115 g/4 oz/ ½ cup of the butter between all the mushrooms.

2 Heat the remaining butter in a frying pan and lightly fry the breadcrumbs until golden brown. Place the chopped parsley in a bowl, add the breadcrumbs, season with salt and cayenne pepper and mix well.

3 Stir in the egg and use the mixture to fill the mushroom caps. Bake for 10–15 minutes until the topping has browned and the mushrooms have softened. Garnish with quartered tomatoes.

COOK'S TIP

If you are planning ahead, stuffed mushrooms can be prepared up to 12 hours in advance and kept in the fridge before baking.

Asparagus Rolls with Herb Butter Sauce

For a taste sensation, try tender asparagus spears wrapped in crisp filo pastry. The buttery herb sauce makes the perfect accompaniment.

INGREDIENTS

Serves 2

4 sheets of filo pastry

50 g/2 oz/¼ cup butter, melted

16 young asparagus spears, trimmed

For the sauce

2 shallots, finely chopped

1 bay leaf

150 ml/¼ pint/⅔ cup dry white wine

175 g/6 oz butter, softened

15 ml/1 tbsp chopped fresh herbs

salt and freshly ground black pepper

chopped chives, to garnish

1 Preheat the oven to 200°C/400°F/Gas 6. Cut the filo sheets in half. Brush a half sheet with melted butter. Fold one corner of the sheet down to the bottom edge to give a wedge shape.

2 Lay 4 asparagus spears on top at the longest edge, and roll up toward the shortest edge. Using the remaining filo and asparagus spears, make three more rolls in the same way.

3 Lay the rolls on a greased baking sheet. Brush with the remaining melted butter. Bake in the oven for 8 minutes until golden brown.

4 Meanwhile, put the shallots, bay leaf and wine into a pan. Cover, and cook over a high heat until the wine is reduced to 45–60 ml/3–4 tbsp.

5 Strain the wine mixture into a bowl. Whisk in the butter, a little at a time until the sauce is smooth and glossy.

6 Stir in the herbs and add salt and pepper to taste. Return to the pan and keep the sauce warm. Serve the rolls on individual plates with a salad garnish, if desired. Serve the sauce separately, sprinkled with a scattering of chopped chives.

Fried Mozzarella

*These crispy cheese slices make an
unusual and tasty starter. They
must be cooked just before serving.*

INGREDIENTS

Serves 2–3

300 g/11 oz/1¾ cups mozzarella cheese

oil for deep frying

2 eggs

flour seasoned with salt and freshly
    ground black pepper

plain dry breadcrumbs

flat leaf parsley, to garnish

1 Cut the mozzarella into slices
about 1 cm/½ in thick. Gently
pat off any excess moisture with
kitchen paper.

2 Heat the oil to 185°C/360°F or
until a small piece of bread
sizzles as soon as it is dropped in.
While the oil is heating, beat the
eggs in a shallow bowl. Spread
some seasoned flour on one plate
and some breadcrumbs on another.

3 Press the cheese slices into the
flour, coating them evenly with
a thin layer of flour. Shake off any
excess. Dip them into the egg, then
once into the breadcrumbs. Dip
them once more into the egg, then
again into the breadcrumbs.

4 Fry immediately in the hot oil
until golden brown. (You may
have to do this in two batches but
do not let the breaded cheese wait
for too long or the breadcrumb
coating will separate from the
cheese while it is being fried.)
Drain on kitchen paper and serve
hot, garnished with parsley.

Greek Cheese and Potato Patties

Delicious little fried morsels of potato and feta cheese, flavoured with dill and lemon juice.

Serves 4

500 g/1¼ lb potatoes

115 g/4 oz feta cheese

4 spring onions, chopped

45 ml/3 tbsp chopped fresh dill

15 ml/1 tbsp lemon juice

1 egg, beaten

flour for dredging

45 ml/3 tbsp olive oil

salt and freshly ground black pepper

1 Boil the potatoes in their skins in lightly salted water until soft. Drain, then peel while still warm. Place in a bowl and mash. Crumble the feta cheese into the potatoes and add the spring onions, dill, lemon juice and egg. Season with salt and pepper (the cheese is salty, so taste before you add salt). Stir well.

2 Cover the mixture and chill until firm. Divide the mixture into walnut-size balls, then flatten them slightly. Dredge with the flour. Heat the oil in a frying pan and fry the patties until golden brown on each side. Drain on kitchen paper and serve at once.

Cheese-stuffed Pears

These pears, with their scrumptious creamy topping, make a sublime dish when served with a simple salad.

INGREDIENTS

Serves 4

50 g/2 oz/¼ cup ricotta cheese

50 g/2 oz/¼ cup dolcelatte cheese

15 ml/1 tbsp honey

½ celery stick, finely sliced

8 green olives, pitted and roughly
    chopped

4 dates, stoned and cut into thin strips

pinch of paprika

4 ripe pears

150 ml/¼ pint/⅔ cup apple juice

1 Preheat the oven to 200°C/400°F/Gas 6. Place the ricotta in a bowl and crumble in the dolcelatte. Add the rest of the ingredients except for the pears and apple juice and mix well.

2 Halve the pears lengthways and use a melon baller to remove the cores. Place in an ovenproof dish and divide the filling equally between them.

3 Pour in the apple juice and cover the dish with foil. Bake for 20 minutes or until the pears are tender.

4 Remove the foil and place the dish under a hot grill for 3 minutes. Serve immediately.

COOK'S TIP

Choose ripe pears in season such as Conference, William or Comice.

Mushroom Croustades

The rich mushroom flavour of this filling is heightened by the addition of mushroom ketchup.

INGREDIENTS

Serves 2–4

1 short French stick, about 25 cm/10 in

10 ml/2 tsp olive oil

250 g/9 oz open cup mushrooms, quartered

10 ml/2 tsp mushroom ketchup

10 ml/2 tsp lemon juice

30 ml/2 tbsp skimmed milk

30 ml/2 tbsp snipped fresh chives

salt and freshly ground black pepper

snipped fresh chives, to garnish

3 Place the mushrooms in a small saucepan with the mushroom ketchup, lemon juice and milk. Simmer for about 5 minutes, or until most of the liquid is evaporated.

4 Remove from the heat, then add the chives and season with salt and pepper. Spoon into the bread croustades and serve hot, garnished with snipped chives.

1 Preheat the oven to 200°C/400°F/Gas 6. Cut the French bread in half lengthways. Cut a scoop out of the soft middle of each half, leaving a thick border all the way round.

2 Brush the bread with oil, place on a baking sheet and bake for about 6–8 minutes, until golden and crisp.

Tomato Pesto Toasties

*The flavour of pesto is so powerful
that it can be used in very small
amounts to good effect, as in these
tasty snacks.*

INGREDIENTS

Serves 2

2 thick slices crusty bread

45 ml/3 tbsp cream cheese or fromage
   frais

10 ml/2 tsp red or green pesto

1 beef tomato

1 red onion

salt and freshly ground black pepper

chopped basil, to garnish

1 Toast the bread slices until
golden brown on both sides.
Leave to cool.

2 Mix together the cheese and
pesto in a small bowl until well
blended, then spread thickly on the
toasted bread.

3 Using a large sharp knife, cut
the beef tomato and red onion
crossways into thin slices.

4 Arrange the tomato and onion
slices, overlapping, on the toast
and season with salt and pepper.
Transfer to a grill rack and heat
through under a hot grill. Serve,
garnished with chopped basil.

COOK'S TIP

Almost any type of crusty bread
can be used for this recipe, but
Italian olive oil bread and French
bread will give the best flavour.

Asparagus with Eggs

The addition of fried eggs and grated Parmesan turns asparagus into something special.

INGREDIENTS

Serves 4

450 g/1 lb fresh asparagus

65 g/2½ oz/5 tbsp butter

4 eggs

60 ml/4 tbsp grated fresh Parmesan cheese

salt and freshly ground black pepper

4 As soon as the asparagus is cooked, remove it from the water with two slotted spoons. Place it on a wire rack covered with a clean dish towel to drain. Divide the spears between warm individual serving plates. Place a fried egg on each and sprinkle with the grated Parmesan.

5 Melt the remaining butter in the frying pan. As soon as it is bubbling, but before it browns, pour it over the cheese and eggs on the asparagus. Season with salt and pepper and serve at once.

1 Cut off any woody ends from the asparagus. Peel the lower half of the spears by inserting a knife under the thick skin at the base and pulling up towards the tip. Wash the asparagus in cold water.

2 Bring a large pan of water to the boil. Boil the asparagus until just tender.

3 While the asparagus is cooking, melt a third of the butter in a frying pan. When bubbling, break in the eggs and cook them until the whites have set but the yolks are still soft.

Curried Eggs

Hard-boiled eggs are served on a bed of mild, creamy sauce with a hint of curry.

Serves 2

4 eggs

15 ml/1 tbsp sunflower oil

1 small onion, finely chopped

2.5 cm/1 in piece of fresh root ginger,
    peeled and grated

2.5 ml/½ tsp ground cumin

2.5 ml/½ tsp garam masala

7.5 ml/1½ tsp tomato paste

10 ml/2 tsp tandoori paste

10 ml/2 tsp lemon juice

250 ml/8 fl oz/¼ cup single cream

15 ml/1 tbsp chopped fresh coriander

salt and freshly ground black pepper

coriander sprigs, to garnish

1 Put the eggs in a pan of water. Bring to the boil, lower the heat and simmer for 10 minutes.

2 Meanwhile, heat the oil in a frying pan. Cook the onion for 2–3 minutes. Add the ginger and cook for 1 minute more.

3 Stir in the ground cumin, garam masala, tomato paste, tandoori paste, lemon juice and cream. Cook for 1–2 minutes, then stir in the coriander. Season with salt and pepper.

4 Drain the eggs, remove the shells and cut each egg in half. Spoon the sauce into a serving bowl, top with the eggs and garnish with coriander sprigs. Serve at once.

Roquefort Tartlets

These can be made in shallow bun tins to serve hot as a first course. You could also make them in tiny cocktail tins, to serve warm as appetizing bite-size snacks with a drink before a meal.

INGREDIENTS

Makes 12

175 g/6 oz/1½ cups plain flour

large pinch of salt

115 g/4 oz/8 tbsp butter

1 egg yolk

30 ml/2 tbsp cold water

For the filling

15 g/½ oz/1 tbsp butter

15 g/½ oz/2 tbsp flour

150 ml/¼ pint/⅔ cup milk

115 g/4 oz Roquefort cheese, crumbled

150 ml/¼ pint/⅔ cup double cream

2.5 ml/½ tsp dried mixed herbs

3 egg yolks

salt and freshly ground black pepper

1 To make the pastry, sift the flour and salt into a bowl and rub the butter into the flour until it resembles breadcrumbs. Mix the egg yolk with the water and stir into the flour to make a soft dough. Knead until smooth, wrap in clear film and chill for 30 minutes. (You can also make the dough in a food processor.)

2 In a saucepan, melt the butter, stir in the flour and then the milk. Boil to thicken, stirring continuously. Off the heat, beat in the cheese and season with salt and pepper. Cool. In another saucepan, bring the cream and herbs to the boil and cook until the liquid has reduced to 30 ml/2 tbsp. Beat into the cheese sauce with the eggs.

3 Preheat the oven to 190°C/375°F/Gas 5. On a lightly floured work surface, roll out the pastry to 3 mm/⅛ in thick. Stamp out rounds with a fluted cutter and use to line your chosen bun tins.

4 Divide the filling between the tartlets; they should be filled or two-thirds full. Stamp out smaller fluted rounds or star shapes for the tops and lay on top of each tartlet. Bake for 20–25 minutes, or until golden brown.

SALADS

Parmesan and Poached Egg Salad

Soft poached eggs, hot garlic croûtons and cool, crisp salad leaves make an unforgettable combination.

INGREDIENTS

Serves 2

½ small loaf
75 ml/5 tbsp olive oil
2 eggs
115 g/4 oz mixed salad leaves
2 garlic cloves, crushed
7 ml/½ tbsp white wine vinegar
25 g/1 oz Parmesan cheese
freshly ground black pepper (optional)

2 Heat 30 ml/2 tbsp of the olive oil in a frying pan. Fry the bread for about 5 minutes, tossing the cubes occasionally, until they are golden brown.

5 Heat the remaining oil in the pan, add the garlic and vinegar, and cook over a high heat for 1 minute. Pour the warm dressing over each salad.

1 Remove the crusts from the bread. Cut the bread into 2.5 cm/1 in cubes.

3 Meanwhile, bring a pan of water to the boil. Carefully slide in the shelled eggs, one at a time. Gently poach the eggs for 4 minutes, until lightly cooked.

6 Place a poached egg on each salad. Sprinkle with shavings of Parmesan and freshly ground black pepper, if using.

4 Divide the salad leaves between two plates. Remove the croûtons from the pan, and arrange them over the leaves. Wipe the pan clean with kitchen paper.

VARIATION

As an alternative to the poached eggs, you could add 40 g/1½ oz/1½ cups of Greek black olives.

COOK'S TIP

Add a dash of vinegar to the water before poaching the eggs. This helps to keep the whites together. To make sure that a poached egg has a good shape, swirl the water with a spoon, whirlpool-fashion, before sliding in the egg.

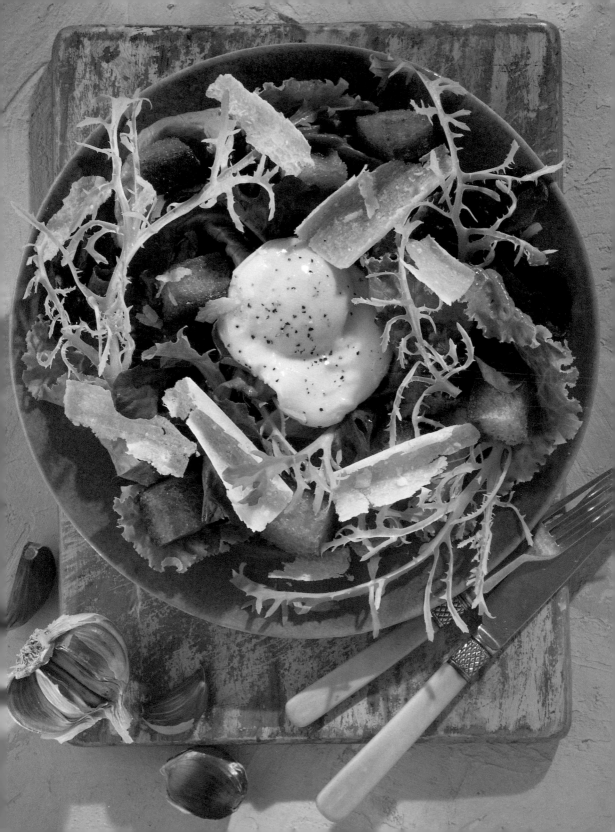

Pear and Pecan Salad with Blue Cheese

Toasted pecan nuts have a special union with crisp white pears. Their robust flavours combine especially well with a rich blue cheese dressing and make this a salad to remember.

INGREDIENTS

Serves 4

75 g/3 oz/½ cup shelled pecan nuts, roughly chopped

3 crisp pears

175 g/6 oz young spinach, stems removed

1 escarole or butterhead lettuce

1 radicchio

30 ml/2 tbsp ready-made blue cheese dressing

salt and freshly ground black pepper

crusty bread, to serve

1 Toast the pecan nuts under a moderate grill, to bring out their flavour.

2 Cut the pears into even slices, leaving the skin intact and discarding the cores.

3 Wash the salad leaves and spin dry. Add the pears together with the toasted pecans, then toss with the dressing. Distribute between 4 large plates and season with salt and pepper. Serve with warm crusty bread.

VARIATION

If you want a lighter non-cheese dressing, combine 5 ml/1 tsp of wholegrain mustard, 2.5 ml/½ tsp of granulated sugar, 1.5 ml/¼ tsp of dried tarragon, 10 ml/2 tsp of lemon juice and 60 ml/4 tbsp of olive oil in a jar and shake vigorously.

New Spring Vegetable Salad

This chunky salad makes a satisfying meal. Use other spring vegetables, if you like.

INGREDIENTS

Serves 4

675 g/1½ lb small new potatoes, halved

400 g/14 oz can broad beans, drained

115 g/4 oz cherry tomatoes

75 g/3 oz/½ cup walnut halves

30 ml/2 tbsp white wine vinegar

15 ml/1 tbsp wholegrain mustard

60 ml/4 tbsp olive oil

pinch of sugar

225 g/8 oz young asparagus
    spears, trimmed

6 spring onions, trimmed

salt and freshly ground black pepper

baby spinach leaves, to serve

1 Put the potatoes in a saucepan. Cover with cold water and bring to the boil. Cook for 10–12 minutes, until tender. Meanwhile, put the broad beans in a bowl. Cut the tomatoes in half and add them to the bowl with the walnuts.

2 Put the white wine vinegar, mustard, olive oil and sugar into a jar. Season with salt and pepper. Close the jar tightly and shake well.

3 Add the asparagus to the potatoes and cook for 3 minutes more. Drain the cooked vegetables well. Cool under cold running water and drain again. Thickly slice the potatoes and cut the spring onions in half.

4 Add the asparagus, potatoes and spring onions to the bowl containing the broad bean mixture. Pour the dressing over the salad and toss well. Serve on a bed of baby spinach leaves.

Couscous Salad

This is a spicy variation on a classic lemon-flavoured tabbouleh, which is traditionally made with bulgur wheat, rather than couscous.

INGREDIENTS

Serves 4

45 ml/3 tbsp olive oil

5 spring onions, chopped

1 garlic clove, crushed

1 tsp ground cumin

350 ml/12 fl oz/1½ cups vegetable stock

175 g/6 oz/1 cup couscous

2 tomatoes, peeled and chopped

60 ml/4 tbsp chopped fresh parsley

60 ml/4 tbsp chopped fresh mint

1 fresh green chilli, seeded and
    finely chopped

30 ml/2 tbsp lemon juice

salt and freshly ground black pepper

toasted pine nuts and grated lemon rind,
    to garnish

crisp lettuce leaves, to serve

1 Heat the oil in a saucepan. Add the spring onions and garlic. Stir in the cumin and cook for 1 minute. Add the stock and bring to the boil.

2 Remove the pan from the heat, stir in the couscous, cover the pan and leave it to stand for 10 minutes, until the couscous has swelled and all the liquid has been absorbed. If you are using instant couscous, follow the package instructions.

3 Tip the couscous into a bowl. Stir in the tomatoes, parsley, mint, chilli and lemon juice. Season with salt and pepper. If possible, leave to stand for up to an hour, to allow the flavours to develop fully.

4 To serve, line a bowl with lettuce leaves and spoon the couscous salad over the top. Scatter the toasted pine nuts and grated lemon rind over the top, to garnish.

Brown Bean Salad

Brown beans, sometimes called 'ful medames', are widely used in Egyptian cooking, and are occasionally seen in health food shops here. Dried broad beans, black or kidney beans make a good substitute.

INGREDIENTS

Serves 6

350 g/12 oz/1½ cups dried brown beans
2 sprigs of fresh thyme
2 bay leaves
1 onion, halved
4 garlic cloves, crushed
2.5 ml/1½ tsp cumin seeds, crushed
3 spring onions, finely chopped
90 ml/6 tbsp chopped fresh parsley
20 ml/4 tsp lemon juice
90 ml/6 tbsp olive oil
3 hard-boiled eggs, shelled and
    roughly chopped
1 pickled cucumber, roughly chopped
salt and freshly ground black pepper

1 Put the beans in a bowl with plenty of cold water and leave to soak overnight. Drain, transfer to a saucepan and cover with fresh water. Bring to the boil and boil rapidly for 10 minutes.

COOK'S TIP
The cooking time for dried beans can vary considerably. They may need only 45 minutes, or a lot longer.

2 Reduce the heat and add the thyme, bay leaves and onion. Simmer very gently for about 1 hour, until tender. Drain and discard the herbs and onion.

3 Mix together the garlic, cumin, spring onions, parsley, lemon juice and oil. Season with salt and pepper. Pour over the beans and toss lightly together. Gently stir in the eggs and cucumber and serve at once.

Pepper and Wild Mushroom Pasta Salad

A combination of grilled peppers and wild mushrooms makes this pasta salad colourful as well as nutritious.

INGREDIENTS

Serves 6

1 red pepper, halved

1 yellow pepper, halved

1 green pepper, halved

350 g/12 oz wholewheat pasta shells
   or twists

30 ml/2 tbsp olive oil

45 ml/3 tbsp balsamic vinegar

75 ml/5 tbsp tomato juice

30 ml/2 tbsp chopped fresh basil

15 ml/1 tbsp chopped fresh thyme

175 g/6 oz shiitake mushrooms, sliced

175 g/6 oz oyster mushrooms, sliced

400 g/14 oz can black-eyed beans, rinsed
   and drained

115 g/4 oz/⅔ cup sultanas

2 bunches spring onions, finely chopped

salt and freshly ground black pepper

1 Preheat the grill. Put the peppers cut-side down on a grill pan rack and place under the hot grill for 10–15 minutes, until the skins are charred. Cover the peppers with a clean, damp dish towel and set aside to cool.

2 Meanwhile, cook the pasta in lightly salted boiling water for 10–12 minutes, until tender, then drain thoroughly.

3 Mix together the oil, vinegar, tomato juice, fresh basil and thyme. Add to the warm pasta and toss together.

4 Remove and discard the skins from the peppers. Seed and slice the peppers and add to the pasta with the mushrooms, beans, sultanas and spring onions. Season with salt and pepper. Toss the ingredients to mix and serve immediately or cover and chill in the fridge before serving.

Wholewheat Pasta Salad

This substantial salad is easily assembled from any combination of seasonal vegetables.

INGREDIENTS

Serves 8

450 g/1 lb short wholewheat pasta, such as fusilli or penne

45 ml/3 tbsp olive oil

2 medium carrots

1 small head broccoli

175 g/6 oz/1 cup shelled peas, fresh or frozen

1 red or yellow pepper, seeded

2 sticks celery

4 spring onions

1 large tomato

75 g/3 oz/½ cup stoned olives

For the dressing

45 ml/3 tbsp wine or balsamic vinegar

60 ml/4 tbsp olive oil

15 ml/1 tbsp Dijon mustard

15 ml/1 tbsp sesame seeds

10 ml/2 tsp chopped mixed fresh herbs such as parsley, thyme and basil

115 g/4 oz/⅔ cup diced Cheddar or mozzarella, or a combination of both

salt and freshly ground black pepper

coriander, to garnish

1 Cook the pasta in a large pan of rapidly boiling salted water until it is tender. Drain and rinse under cold water to stop the cooking.

2 Drain well and turn into a large bowl. Toss with 45 ml/ 3 tbsp of the olive oil and set aside. Allow to cool completely before mixing with the other ingredients.

3 Lightly blanch the carrots, broccoli and peas in a large pan of boiling water. Refresh under cold water. Drain well.

4 Chop the carrots and broccoli into bite-size pieces and add to the pasta with the peas. Slice the pepper, celery, spring onions and tomato into small pieces. Add them to the salad with the olives.

5 Make the dressing in a small bowl by combining the vinegar with the oil and mustard. Stir in the sesame seeds and herbs. Mix the dressing into the salad. Taste for seasoning, add salt and pepper or more oil and vinegar as necessary. Stir in the cheese. Allow the salad to stand for 15 minutes before serving. Garnish with coriander.

Fruity Rice Salad

An appetizing and colourful rice salad combining many different flavours, ideal for a packed lunch.

INGREDIENTS

Serves 4–6

225 g/8 oz/1 cup mixed brown and
  wild rice
1 yellow pepper, seeded and diced
1 bunch spring onions, chopped
3 sticks celery, chopped
1 large beefsteak tomato, chopped
2 green-skinned eating apples, chopped
175 g/6 oz/¾ cup ready-to-eat dried
  apricots, chopped
115 g/4 oz/⅔ cup raisins
30 ml/2 tbsp unsweetened apple juice
30 ml/2 tbsp dry sherry
30 ml/2 tbsp light soy sauce
dash of Tabasco sauce
30 ml/2 tbsp chopped fresh parsley
15 ml/1 tbsp chopped fresh rosemary
salt and freshly ground black pepper

2 Place the pepper, spring onions, celery, tomato, apples, apricots, raisins and the cooked rice in a serving bowl and mix well.

3 In a small bowl, mix together the apple juice, sherry, soy sauce, Tabasco sauce and herbs. Season with salt and pepper.

4 Pour the dressing over the rice mixture and toss the ingredients together to mix. Serve immediately or cover and chill in the fridge before serving.

1 Cook the rice in a large saucepan of lightly salted boiling water for about 30 minutes (or according to the package instructions) until tender. Rinse the cooked rice under cold running water to cool quickly, and drain thoroughly.

Marinated Cucumber Salad

Sprinkling the cucumber with salt draws out some of the water and makes them crisper.

INGREDIENTS

Serves 4–6

2 medium cucumbers

15 ml/1 tbsp salt

90 g/3½ oz/½ cup granulated sugar

175 ml/6 fl oz/¾ cup dry cider

15 ml/1 tbsp cider vinegar

45 ml/3 tbsp chopped fresh dill

pinch of freshly ground black pepper

sprig of dill, to garnish

1 Slice the cucumbers thinly and place them in a colander, sprinkling salt between each layer. Put the colander over a bowl and leave to drain for 1 hour.

2 Thoroughly rinse the cucumber slices under cold running water to remove excess salt, then pat dry on absorbent kitchen paper.

3 Gently heat the sugar, cider and vinegar in a saucepan, until the sugar has dissolved. Remove from the heat and leave to cool. Put the cucumber slices in a bowl, pour over the cider mixture and leave to marinate for 2 hours.

4 Drain the cucumber and sprinkle with the dill and pepper to taste. Mix well and transfer to a serving dish. Garnish with a sprig of dill. Chill in the fridge until ready to serve.

Classic Greek Salad

If you have ever visited Greece, you'll know that a Greek salad with a chunk of bread makes a delicious, filling meal.

INGREDIENTS

Serves 4

1 romaine lettuce
½ cucumber, halved lengthwise
4 tomatoes
8 spring onions
50 g/2 oz/⅓ cup Greek black olives
115 g/4 oz feta cheese
90 ml/6 tbsp white wine vinegar
120 ml/4 fl oz/½ cup olive oil
salt and freshly ground black pepper
olives and bread, to serve (optional)

3 Slice the spring onions. Add them to the bowl with the olives and toss well.

4 Cut the feta cheese into cubes and add to the salad.

5 Put the vinegar, olive oil and salt and pepper into a small bowl and whisk well. Pour the dressing over the salad and toss to combine. Serve at once, with olives and chunks of bread, if desired.

1 Tear the lettuce into pieces, and place them in a large mixing bowl. Slice the cucumber and add to the bowl.

2 Cut the tomatoes into wedges and put them into the bowl.

COOK'S TIP

The salad can be assembled in advance and chilled, but add the lettuce and dressing just before serving. Keep the dressing at room temperature, as chilling deadens its flavour.

Fresh Spinach and Avocado Salad

Young, tender spinach leaves make a change from lettuce and are delicious served with avocado, cherry tomatoes and radishes in a tofu sauce.

Serves 2–3

1 large avocado
juice of 1 lime
225 g/8 oz fresh baby spinach leaves
115 g/4 oz cherry tomatoes
4 spring onions, sliced
½ cucumber
50 g/2 oz radishes, sliced

For the dressing
115 g/4 oz soft silken tofu
45 ml/3 tbsp milk
10 ml/2 tsp prepared mustard
2.5 ml/½ tsp white wine vinegar
pinch of cayenne, plus extra to serve
salt and freshly ground black pepper

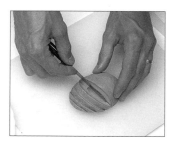

1 Cut the avocado in half, remove the stone, and strip off the skin. Cut the flesh into slices. Transfer to a plate, drizzle over the lime juice, and set aside.

COOK'S TIP

Use soft, silken tofu rather than the firm block variety. It can be found in most supermarkets in long-life cartons.

2 Wash and dry the spinach leaves. Put them in a mixing bowl.

3 Cut the larger cherry tomatoes in half, and add all the tomatoes to the mixing bowl, with the spring onions. Cut the cucumber into chunks, and add to the bowl with the sliced radishes.

4 Make the dressing. Put the tofu, milk, mustard, wine vinegar and cayenne in a food processor or blender. Add salt and pepper to taste. Process for 30 seconds until smooth. Scrape the dressing into a bowl, and add a little extra milk if you like a thinner dressing. Sprinkle with a little extra cayenne, and garnish with radish roses and herb sprigs.

Sweet and Sour Peppers with Pasta Bows

A zesty dressing makes this simple pasta salad really special.

INGREDIENTS

Serves 4–6

1 each red, yellow and orange pepper

1 garlic clove, crushed

30 ml/2 tbsp capers

30 ml/2 tbsp raisins

5 ml/1 tsp wholegrain mustard

grated rind and juice of 1 lime

5 ml/1 tsp runny honey

30 ml/2 tbsp chopped fresh coriander

225 g/8 oz pasta bows

salt and freshly ground black pepper

shavings of Parmesan cheese, to
    serve (optional)

1 Quarter the peppers and remove the stalks and seeds. Put into boiling water and cook for 10–15 minutes, until tender. Drain and rinse under cold water. Peel away the skins and seeds and cut the flesh lengthways into strips.

2 Put the garlic, capers, raisins, mustard, lime rind and juice, honey and coriander into a bowl. Season with salt and pepper and whisk together.

3 Cook the pasta in a large pan of boiling salted water for 10–12 minutes, until tender. Drain thoroughly.

4 Return the pasta to the pan, add the peppers and dressing. Heat gently and toss to mix. Transfer to a warm serving bowl. Serve with a few shavings of Parmesan cheese, if using.

Bulgur Wheat and Broad Bean Salad

This appetizing salad is ideal served with fresh crusty wholemeal bread and home-made chutney or pickle.

INGREDIENTS

Serves 6

350 g/12 oz/2 cups bulgur wheat
225 g/8 oz frozen broad beans
115 g/4 oz/1 cup frozen petit pois
225 g/8 oz cherry tomatoes, halved
1 Spanish onion, chopped
1 red pepper, seeded and chopped
50 g/2 oz mangetouts, chopped
50 g/2 oz watercress
15 ml/1 tbsp chopped fresh parsley
15 ml/1 tbsp chopped fresh basil
15 ml/1 tbsp chopped fresh thyme
French dressing
salt and freshly ground black pepper

3 Add the cherry tomatoes, onion, pepper, mangetouts and watercress to the bulgur wheat mixture. Toss well together in the bowl until all the ingredients are well-combined.

4 Add the chopped fresh parsley, basil and thyme and French dressing to taste. Season with salt and pepper and toss the ingredients together. Serve immediately or cover and chill in the refrigerator before serving.

1 Soak and cook the bulgur wheat according to the package instructions. Drain thoroughly and put into a serving bowl.

2 Meanwhile, cook the broad beans and petit pois in boiling water for 3 minutes. Drain and add to the prepared bulgur wheat.

COOK'S TIP

Use cooked couscous, boiled brown rice or wholewheat pasta in place of the bulgur wheat.

Sweet and Sour Artichoke Salad

Agrodolce is a sweet and sour sauce which works perfectly in this salad.

INGREDIENTS

Serves 4

6 small globe artichokes

juice of 1 lemon

30 ml/2 tbsp olive oil

2 medium onions, roughly chopped

175 g/6 oz/1 cup fresh or frozen broad
beans (shelled weight)

175 g/6 oz/1½ cups fresh or frozen peas
(shelled weight)

salt and freshly ground black pepper

fresh mint leaves, to garnish

For the salsa agrodolce

120 ml/4 fl oz/½ cup white wine vinegar

15 ml/1 tbsp caster sugar

handful fresh mint leaves, roughly torn

1 Peel the outer leaves from the artichokes and cut into quarters. Place them in a bowl of water with the lemon juice.

2 Heat the oil in a large saucepan and cook the onions until golden. Add the beans and stir.

3 Drain the artichokes and add them to the pan. Pour in about 300 ml/½ pint/1¼ cups of water and cover. Simmer gently for 10–15 minutes.

4 Add the peas, season with salt and pepper and cook for a further 5 minutes, stirring from time to time, until the vegetables are tender.

5 Strain the vegetables through a sieve and place them in a bowl. Leave to cool, then cover and chill in the refrigerator.

6 To make the salsa, mix all the ingredients in a pan. Heat gently until the sugar has dissolved. Simmer for 5 minutes. Leave to cool. Drizzle over the salad. Garnish with mint leaves.

Spanish Asparagus and Orange Salad

Complicated salad dressings are rarely found in Spain – they simply rely on the wonderful flavour of a good quality olive oil.

INGREDIENTS

Serves 4

225 g/8 oz asparagus, trimmed and cut
    into 5 cm/2 in pieces
2 large oranges
2 tomatoes, cut into eighths
50 g/2 oz romaine lettuce leaves, shredded
30 ml/2 tbsp olive oil
2.5 ml/½ tsp sherry vinegar
salt and freshly ground black pepper

1 Cook the asparagus in boiling salted water for 3–4 minutes, until just tender. Drain and refresh under cold water.

2 Grate the rind from half an orange and reserve. Peel both the oranges and cut into segments. Squeeze out the juice from the membrane and reserve the juice.

3 Put the asparagus, orange segments, tomatoes and lettuce into a salad bowl. Mix together the oil and vinegar and add 15 ml/1 tbsp of the reserved orange juice and 2.5 ml/1 tsp of the rind. Season the dressing with salt and pepper. Just before serving, pour the dressing over the salad and mix gently to coat.

COOK'S TIP

Cos or Little Gem lettuce can be used in place of romaine.

Grilled Goat's Cheese Salad

Here is the salad and cheese course on one plate – or serve it as a quick and satisfying starter or light lunch. The fresh tangy flavour of goat's cheese contrasts with the mild salad leaves.

INGREDIENTS

Serves 4

2 firm round whole goat's cheeses, such as
    Crottin de Chavignol (about
    65–115 g/2½–4 oz each)
4 slices French bread
olive oil, for drizzling
175 g/6 oz mixed salad leaves, including
    soft and bitter varieties
snipped fresh chives, to garnish

For the dressing
½ clove garlic
5 ml/1 tsp Dijon mustard
5 ml/1 tsp white wine vinegar
5 ml/1 tsp dry white wine
45 ml/3 tbsp olive oil
salt and freshly ground black pepper

1 To make the dressing, rub a large salad bowl with the cut side of the garlic clove. Combine the mustard, vinegar, wine, salt and pepper in a bowl. Whisk in the oil, 15 ml/1 tbsp at a time, to form a thick vinaigrette.

2 Cut the goat's cheeses in half crossways using a sharp knife.

3 Preheat the grill to hot. Arrange the bread slices on a baking sheet and toast on one side. Turn over and place a piece of cheese, cut side up, on each slice. Drizzle with oil and grill until the cheese is lightly browned.

4 Add the leaves and the dressing to the salad bowl and toss to coat the leaves thoroughly. Divide the salad among four plates, top each with a goat's cheese croûton and serve, garnished with chives.

Tomato and Feta Cheese Salad

Sweet sun-ripened tomatoes are rarely more delicious than when served with feta cheese and olive oil. This salad, popular in Greece and Turkey, is enjoyed as a light meal with pieces of crispy bread.

INGREDIENTS

Serves 4

900 g/2 lb tomatoes

200 g/7 oz feta cheese

120 ml/4 fl oz/½ cup olive oil, preferably
   Greek

12 black olives

4 sprigs of fresh basil

freshly ground black pepper

1 Remove the tough cores from the tomatoes with a small sharp knife.

COOK'S TIP

Feta cheese has a strong flavour and can be salty. The least salty variety is imported from Greece and Turkey and is available from specialist delicatessens.

2 Slice the tomatoes thickly and arrange in a shallow dish.

3 Crumble the cheese over the tomatoes, sprinkle with olive oil, then strew with olives and fresh basil. Season with black pepper and serve at room temperature.

Fennel, Orange and Rocket Salad

This light and refreshing salad is the ideal companion for spicy or rich foods.

INGREDIENTS

Serves 4

2 oranges

1 fennel bulb

115 g/4 oz rocket leaves

50 g/2 oz/⅓ cup black olives

For the dressing

30 ml/2 tbsp olive oil

15 ml/1 tbsp balsamic vinegar

1 small garlic clove, crushed

salt and freshly ground black pepper

1 With a vegetable peeler, cut strips of rind from the oranges, leaving the pith behind.

2 Cut the strips into thin julienne strips. Cook in boiling water for a few minutes. Drain.

3 Peel the oranges, removing all the white pith. Cut the orange flesh crossways into thin rounds and discard any pips.

4 Cut the fennel bulb in half lengthways and slice across the bulb as thinly as possible. It is easier to do this with a food processor fitted with a slicing disk or using a mandoline.

5 Combine the oranges and fennel in a serving bowl and toss with the rocket leaves.

6 Mix together the oil, vinegar, garlic and seasoning and pour over the salad. Toss together well and leave to stand for a few minutes. Sprinkle with the black olives and julienne strips of orange peel.

Aubergine, Lemon and Caper Salad

This cooked vegetable relish is delicious served with pasta or simply on its own with crusty bread.

INGREDIENTS

Serves 4

1 large aubergine, about 675 g/1½ lb

5 ml/1 tsp salt

60 ml/4 tbsp olive oil

grated rind and juice of 1 lemon

30 ml/2 tbsp capers, rinsed

12 stoned green olives

1 small garlic clove, chopped

30 ml/2 tbsp chopped fresh flat leaf parsley

salt and freshly ground black pepper

1 Cut the aubergine into 2.5 cm/1 in cubes. Place the cubes in a colander and sprinkle over the salt. Set aside for 30 minutes, then rinse thoroughly under cold running water. Pat dry with kitchen paper.

2 Heat the olive oil in a large frying pan. Cook the aubergine cubes over medium heat for about 10 minutes, tossing regularly, until golden and softened. You may need to do this in two batches to ensure that all the aubergine cubes brown well. Drain on kitchen paper and season with a little salt.

3 Place the aubergine cubes in a large serving bowl, toss with the lemon rind and juice, capers, olives, garlic and chopped parsley.

4 Season with salt and pepper. Serve at room temperature.

> ### COOK'S TIP
>
>
> This will taste even better when made the day before. It will keep, covered in the fridge, for up to 4 days. To enrich this dish to serve on its own as a main course, add toasted pine nuts and shavings of Parmesan cheese. Serve with crusty bread.

Rocket, Pear and Parmesan Salad

For a sophisticated start to an elaborate meal, try this simple salad of honey-rich pears, fresh Parmesan and aromatic leaves of rocket.

INGREDIENTS

Serves 4

3 ripe pears, Williams or Packhams

10 ml/2 tsp lemon juice

45 ml/3 tbsp hazelnut or walnut oil

115 g/4 oz rocket

75 g/3 oz Parmesan cheese

freshly ground black pepper

open-textured bread, to serve

1 Peel and core the pears and slice thickly. Moisten with lemon juice to keep the flesh white.

2 Combine the nut oil with the pears. Add the rocket leaves and toss.

3 Turn the salad out on to 4 small plates and top with shavings of Parmesan cheese. Season with freshly ground black pepper and serve with open-textured bread.

COOK'S TIP

If you are unable to buy rocket easily, you can grow your own from early spring to late summer.

Tomato, Spring Onion and Coriander Salad

Known as Cachumbar, this salad relish is most commonly served with Indian curries. There are many versions, and this one will leave your mouth feeling cool and fresh after a spicy meal.

Serves 4

3 ripe tomatoes

2 spring onions, chopped

1.5 ml/¼ tsp caster sugar

45 ml/3 tbsp chopped fresh coriander

salt

2 Halve the tomatoes, remove the seeds and dice the flesh.

3 Combine the tomatoes with the spring onions, sugar, chopped coriander and salt. Serve at room temperature.

1 Remove the tough cores from the tomatoes with a small sharp knife.

COOK'S TIP

This refreshing salad also makes a fine filler for pitta bread with hummus.

SIDE DISHES

Sautéed Potatoes

These rosemary-scented, crisp golden potatoes are a favourite in French households.

INGREDIENTS

Serves 6

1.3 kg/3 lb baking potatoes

60–90 ml/4–6 tbsp oil or clarified butter

2 or 3 sprigs of fresh rosemary, leaves
    removed and chopped

salt and freshly ground black pepper

1 Peel the potatoes and cut into
2.5 cm/1 in pieces. Place them
in a bowl, cover with cold water
and leave to soak for 10–15
minutes. Drain, rinse and drain
again, then dry thoroughly in a
dish towel.

2 Heat about 60 ml/4 tbsp of the
oil or butter over a medium-
high heat, until very hot but not
smoking. Add the potatoes and
cook for 2 minutes without
stirring, so that they seal completely and brown on one side.

3 Shake the pan and toss the
potatoes to brown on another
side. Season with salt and pepper.

4 Add a little more oil or butter
and continue cooking the
potatoes over medium-low to low
heat for 20–25 minutes, until
tender when pierced with a knife,
stirring and shaking the pan
frequently. About 5 minutes before
the end of cooking, sprinkle the
potatoes with the chopped
rosemary.

Straw Potato Cake

*These fried grated potatoes resemble
straw, hence the name of the recipe.
You could make several small cakes
instead of a large one, if you prefer –
simply adjust the cooking time
accordingly.*

INGREDIENTS

Serves 4

450 g/1 lb baking potatoes

25 ml/1½ tbsp melted butter

15 ml/1 tbsp vegetable oil, plus more
    if needed

salt and freshly ground black pepper

1 Peel the potatoes and grate
them coarsely, then immediately toss them with melted butter
and season with salt and pepper.

2 Heat the oil in a large frying
pan. Add the potato mixture
and press down to form an even
layer that covers the pan. Cook
over a medium heat for 7–10
minutes until the base is well
browned.

3 Loosen the potato cake by
shaking the pan or running a
thin palette knife under it.

4 To turn the potato cake over,
invert a large baking tray over
the frying pan and, holding it
tightly against the pan, turn them
both over together. Lift off the
frying pan, return it to the heat
and add a little oil if it looks dry.
Slide the potato cake into the
frying pan and continue cooking
until crisp and browned on both
sides. Serve hot.

Puffy Creamed Potatoes

This accompaniment consists of creamed potatoes incorporated into mini Yorkshire puddings. Serve them with a vegetable casserole or, for a meal on its own, serve two or three per person and accompany with salads.

INGREDIENTS

Makes 6

275 g/10 oz potatoes

creamy milk and butter for mashing

5 ml/1 tsp chopped fresh parsley

5 ml/1 tsp chopped fresh tarragon

75 g/3 oz/⅔ cup plain flour

1 egg

about 120 ml/4 fl oz/½ cup milk

oil or sunflower margarine, for baking

salt and freshly ground black pepper

1 Boil the potatoes until tender and mash with a little milk and butter. Stir in the chopped parsley and tarragon and season with salt and pepper. Preheat the oven to 200°C/400°F/Gas 6.

2 Process the flour, egg, milk and a pinch of salt in a food processor or blender to make a smooth batter.

3 Place about 2.5 ml/½ tsp oil or a small knob of sunflower margarine in each of six ramekin dishes and place in the oven on a baking tray for 2–3 minutes, until the oil or fat is very hot.

4 Working quickly, pour a small amount of batter (about 20 ml/4 tsp) into each ramekin dish. Add a heaped tablespoon of mashed potatoes and then pour an equal amount of the remaining batter in each dish. Place in the oven and bake for 15–20 minutes, until the puddings are puffy and golden brown.

5 Using a palette knife, carefully ease the puddings out of the ramekin dishes and arrange on a large warm serving dish. Serve at once.

Potatoes Dauphinois

Rich, creamy and satisfying, this is a really comforting dish to serve when it's cold outside.

Serves 4

675 g/1½ lb potatoes, peeled and
   thinly sliced
1 garlic clove
25 g/1 oz/2 tbsp butter
300 ml/½ pint/1¼ cups single cream
50 ml/2 fl oz/¼ cup milk
salt and white pepper

1 Preheat the oven to 150°C/300°F/Gas 2. Place the potato slices in a bowl of cold water to remove the excess starch. Drain and pat dry with kitchen paper.

2 Cut the garlic in half and rub the cut side around the inside of a wide shallow ovenproof dish. Butter the dish generously. Blend the cream and milk in a jug.

3 Cover the base of the dish with a layer of potatoes. Dot a little butter over the potato layer, season with salt and pepper and then pour over a little of the cream and milk mixture.

4 Continue making layers, until all the ingredients have been used up, ending with a layer of cream. Bake in the oven for about 1¼ hours. If the dish browns too quickly, cover with a lid or with a piece of foil. The potatoes are ready when they are very soft and the top is golden brown.

Spicy Potatoes and Cauliflower

This dish is simplicity itself to make and can be eaten as a main meal with Indian breads or rice, a raita such as cucumber and yogurt, and a fresh mint relish.

INGREDIENTS

Serves 2

225 g/8 oz potatoes

75 ml/5 tbsp peanut oil

5 ml/1 tsp ground cumin

5 ml/1 tsp ground coriander

1.5 ml/¼ tsp ground turmeric

1.5 ml/¼ tsp cayenne pepper

1 fresh green chilli, seeded and finely chopped

1 medium cauliflower, broken up into small florets

5 ml/1 tsp cumin seeds

2 garlic cloves, cut into shreds

15–30 ml/1–2 tbsp fresh coriander, finely chopped

salt

1 Cook the potatoes in their skins in boiling salted water for about 20 minutes, until just tender. Drain and let cool. When cool enough to handle, peel and cut into 2.5 cm/1 in cubes.

2 Heat 45 ml/3 tbsp of the oil in a frying pan or wok. When hot, add the ground cumin, coriander, turmeric, cayenne pepper and chilli. Let the spices sizzle for a few seconds.

3 Add the cauliflower and about 60 ml/4 tbsp water. Cook over medium heat, stirring continuously, for 6–8 minutes. Add the potatoes and stir-fry for 2–3 minutes. Season with salt, then remove from the heat.

4 Heat the remaining oil in a small frying pan. When hot, add the cumin seeds and garlic and cook until lightly browned. Pour the mixture over the vegetables. Sprinkle with the chopped coriander and serve at once.

Garlic Mashed Potatoes

These creamy mashed potatoes have a wonderful aroma. Although two bulbs seems like a lot of garlic, the flavour is sweet and subtle when cooked in this way.

INGREDIENTS

Serves 6–8

2 garlic bulbs, separated into cloves, unpeeled

115 g/4 oz/½ cup unsalted butter

1.3 kg/3 lb baking potatoes

120–175 ml/4–6 fl oz/½–¾ cup milk

salt and white pepper

1 Bring a small saucepan of water to the boil over high heat. Add the garlic cloves and boil for 2 minutes, then drain and peel.

2 In a heavy frying pan, melt half of the butter over a low heat. Add the blanched garlic cloves, then cover and cook gently for 20–25 minutes, until very tender and just golden, shaking the pan and stirring occasionally. Do not allow the garlic to scorch or brown.

3 Remove the pan from the heat and cool slightly. Spoon the garlic and any butter from the pan into a blender or food processor fitted with a metal blade and process until smooth. Tip into a small bowl, press clear film on to the surface to prevent a skin forming and set aside.

4 Peel and quarter the potatoes, place in a large saucepan and add enough cold water to just cover them. Salt the water generously and bring to the boil over a high heat.

5 Cook the potatoes until tender, then drain and work through a food mill or press through a sieve back into the saucepan. Return the pan to a medium heat and, using a wooden spoon, stir the potatoes for 1–2 minutes to dry them out completely. Remove from the heat.

6 Warm the milk over a medium-high heat until bubbles form around the edge. Gradually beat the milk, remaining butter and reserved garlic purée into the potatoes, then season with salt, if needed, and white pepper.

Roasted Potatoes, Peppers and Shallots

This popular dish from North America's Deep South is often served in elegant New Orleans restaurants.

INGREDIENTS

Serves 4

500 g/1¼ lb waxy potatoes

2 sweet yellow peppers

12 shallots

olive oil

2 sprigs of fresh rosemary

salt and freshly ground black pepper

1 Preheat the oven to 200°C/400°F/Gas 6. Wash the potatoes and blanch for 5 minutes in boiling water. Drain.

2 When the potatoes are cool enough to handle, skin them and halve lengthways. Cut each sweet pepper lengthways into 8 strips, discarding the seeds and pith.

3 Peel the shallots, allowing them to fall into their natural segments.

4 Oil a shallow ovenproof dish thoroughly with olive oil.

5 Arrange the potatoes and peppers in alternating rows and stud with the shallots.

6 Cut the rosemary sprigs into 5 cm/2 in lengths and tuck among the vegetables. Season the dish generously with olive oil, salt and pepper and bake in the oven, uncovered, for 30–40 minutes, until all the vegetables are tender.

Baked Sweet Potatoes

*Give sweet potatoes a Cajun flavour
with salt, three different kinds of
pepper and lavish quantities of
butter. Serve half a potato per
person as an accompaniment, or a
whole one as a supper dish with
a green salad peppered with
watercress.*

INGREDIENTS

Serves 3–6

3 pink-skinned sweet potatoes, about
   450 g/1 lb each
75 g/3 oz/6 tbsp butter, sliced
black, white and cayenne peppers
salt

1 Wash the potatoes and leave
  the skins wet. Rub salt into the
skins, prick them all over with a
fork and place on the middle shelf
of the oven. Turn on the oven to
200°C/400°F/Gas 6 and bake for
about an hour, until the flesh
yields and feels soft when pressed.

COOK'S TIP

Sweet potatoes cook more
quickly than ordinary ones, and
there is no need to preheat
the oven.

---

2 The potatoes can either be
  served in halves or whole. For
halves, split each one lengthways
and make close criss-cross cuts in
the flesh of each half. Then spread
with slices of butter, and work the
butter and seasonings roughly into
the cuts with a knife point.

3 Alternatively, make an incision
  along the length of each potato
if they are to be served whole.
Open them slightly and put in
butter slices along the length,
seasoning with the peppers and a
pinch of salt.

Thai Fragrant Rice

This lovely, soft, fluffy rice dish, perfumed with fresh lemon grass, is a classic Thai accompaniment to red and green curries.

INGREDIENTS

Serves 4

1 stalk of lemon grass

2 limes

225 g/8 oz/1 cup brown basmati rice

15 ml/1 tbsp olive oil

1 onion, chopped

2.5 cm/1 in piece of fresh root ginger, peeled and finely chopped

7.5ml/1½ tsp coriander seeds

7.5 ml/1½ tsp cumin seeds

750 ml/1¼ pints/3 cups vegetable stock

60 ml/4 tbsp chopped fresh coriander

lime wedges, to serve

1 Finely chop the lemon grass using a sharp knife.

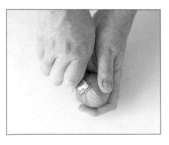

2 Remove the zest from the limes using a zester or fine grater. Avoid removing the pith with the zest.

3 Rinse the rice in plenty of cold water until the water runs clear. Drain through a sieve.

4 Heat the oil in a large pan and add the onion, spices, lemon grass and lime zest and cook gently for 2–3 minutes.

COOK'S TIP

Other varieties of rice, such as white basmati or long grain, can be used for this dish, but you will need to adjust the cooking times accordingly.

5 Add the rice and cook for another minute, then add the stock and bring to the boil. Reduce the heat to very low and cover the pan. Cook gently for 30 minutes then check the rice. If it is still crunchy, cover the pan again and leave for a further 3–5 minutes. Remove from the heat.

6 Stir in the chopped fresh coriander, fluff up the grains, cover and leave for 10 minutes. Serve with lime wedges.

Rice with Seeds and Spices

A change from plain boiled rice, and a colourful accompaniment to serve with spicy curries. Basmati rice gives the best texture and flavour, but you can use ordinary long grain rice instead, if you prefer.

INGREDIENTS

Serves 4

5 ml/1 tsp sunflower oil

2.5 ml/½ tsp ground turmeric

6 cardamom pods, lightly crushed

5 ml/1 tsp coriander seeds, lightly crushed

1 garlic clove, crushed

200 g/7 oz/1 cup basmati rice

400 ml/14 fl oz/1⅔ cups vegetable stock

115 g/4 oz/½ cup natural yogurt

15 ml/1 tbsp toasted sunflower seeds

15 ml/1 tbsp toasted sesame seeds

salt and freshly ground black pepper

coriander leaves, to garnish

2 Add the rice and stock, bring to the boil, then cover and simmer for 15 minutes, or until just tender.

3 Stir in the yogurt and the toasted sunflower and sesame seeds. Season with salt and pepper and serve hot, garnished with coriander leaves.

1 Heat the oil in a non-stick frying pan and fry the spices and garlic for about 1 minute, stirring all the time.

COOK'S TIP

Seeds are particularly rich in minerals, so they are a good addition to all kinds of dishes. Light toasting will improve their flavour.

Red Fried Rice

*This vibrant rice dish owes its
appeal as much to the bright colours
of red onion, red pepper and
tomatoes as it does to their flavours.*

INGREDIENTS

Serves 2

145 g/4½ oz/¾ cup basmati rice

30 ml/2 tbsp peanut oil

1 small red onion, chopped

1 red pepper, seeded and chopped

225 g/8 oz cherry tomatoes, halved

2 eggs, beaten

salt and freshly ground black pepper

1 Wash the rice several times
under cold running water.
Drain well. Bring a large pan of
water to the boil. Add the rice and
cook for 10–12 minutes.

2 Meanwhile, heat the oil in a
wok until very hot. Add the
onion and red pepper and stir-fry
for 2–3 minutes. Add the cherry
tomatoes and continue stir-frying
for 2 minutes more.

3 Pour in the beaten eggs all at
once. Cook for 30 seconds
without stirring, then stir to break
up the egg as it sets.

4 Drain the cooked rice thoroughly. Add to the wok and
toss it over the heat with the vegetables and egg mixture for 3
minutes. Season with salt and
pepper and serve immediately.

Herby Rice Pilaf

A quick and easy recipe to make, this simple pilaf is delicious to eat. Serve with a selection of fresh seasonal vegetables such as broccoli florets, baby sweetcorn and carrots.

INGREDIENTS

Serves 4

225 g/8 oz mixed brown basmati and
    wild rice

15 ml/1 tbsp olive oil

1 onion, chopped

1 garlic clove, crushed

5 ml/1 tsp ground cumin

5 ml/1 tsp ground turmeric

50 g/2 oz/½ cup sultanas

750 ml/1¼ pints/3 cups vegetable stock

30–45 ml/2–3 tbsp chopped fresh
    mixed herbs

salt and freshly ground black pepper

sprigs of fresh herbs and 25 g/1 oz/¼ cup
    pistachio nuts, chopped, to garnish

1 Wash the rice under cold running water, then drain well. Heat the oil, add the onion and garlic and cook gently for 5 minutes, stirring occasionally.

2 Add the spices and rice and cook gently for 1 minute, stirring. Stir in the sultanas and stock, bring to the boil, cover and simmer gently for 20–25 minutes, stirring occasionally.

3 Stir in the chopped mixed herbs and season with salt and pepper. Spoon the pilaf into a warmed serving dish and garnish with fresh herb sprigs and a scattering of chopped pistachio nuts. Serve immediately.

Cheese-topped Roast Baby Vegetables

This is a simple way to bring out the real flavour of baby vegetables.

INGREDIENTS

Serves 6

1 kg/2¼ lb mixed baby vegetables, such
    as aubergines, onions or shallots,
    courgettes, sweetcorn, button
    mushrooms

1 red pepper, seeded and cut into large
    chunks

1–2 garlic cloves, finely chopped

15-30 ml/1–2 tbsp olive oil

30 ml/2 tbsp chopped fresh mixed herbs

225 g/8 oz cherry tomatoes

115 g/4 oz/1 cup mozzarella cheese,
    coarsely grated

salt and freshly ground black pepper

black olives, to garnish (optional)

1 Preheat the oven to 220°C/425°F/Gas 7. Cut the aubergines and onions or shallots in half lengthways.

2 Place the baby vegetables, red pepper and garlic in a shallow ovenproof dish. Season with salt and pepper, drizzle over the oil and toss the vegetables to coat. Bake for 20 minutes, until tinged brown at the edges, stirring once.

3 Stir in the herbs, scatter over the tomatoes and top with the mozzarella cheese. Bake for a further 5-10 minutes, until the cheese has melted and is bubbling. Serve at once, garnished with black olives, if using.

Chinese Brussels Sprouts

If you are bored with plain boiled Brussels sprouts, try pepping them up Chinese-style with this unusual stir-fried method.

INGREDIENTS

Serves 4

450 g/1 lb Brussels sprouts

5 ml/1 tsp sesame or sunflower oil

2 spring onions, sliced

2.5 ml/½ tsp Chinese five-spice powder

15 ml/1 tbsp light soy sauce

1 Trim the Brussels sprouts, then shred them finely using a large sharp knife or a food processor.

2 Heat the oil and add the sprouts and spring onions. Stir-fry for about 2 minutes, without allowing the mixture to brown.

3 Stir in the five-spice powder and soy sauce, then cook, stirring, for a further 2–3 minutes, until just tender. Serve hot with other Chinese dishes.

Festive Brussels Sprouts

This recipe originated in France, where it is a popular side dish at Christmas time.

INGREDIENTS

Serves 4 6

225 g/8 oz chestnuts

120 ml/4 fl oz/½ cup milk

500 g/1¼ lb/4 cups small tender
  Brussels sprouts

25 g/1 oz/2 tbsp butter

1 shallot, finely chopped

30-45 ml/2–3 tbsp dry white wine
  or water

1 Using a small knife, score a cross in the base of each chestnut. Bring a saucepan of water to the boil over medium-high heat, then drop in the chestnuts and boil for 6–8 minutes. Remove pan from the heat.

2 Using a slotted spoon, remove a few chestnuts from the pan, leaving the others immersed in the water until ready to peel. Before the chestnuts cool, remove the outer shell with a knife and then peel off the inner skin.

3 Rinse the pan, return the peeled chestnuts to it and add the milk. Top up with enough water to completely cover the chestnuts. Simmer over medium heat for 12–15 minutes until the chestnuts are just tender. Drain and set aside.

4 Remove any wilted or yellow leaves from the Brussels sprouts. Trim the root ends but leave intact or the leaves will separate. Using a small knife, score a cross in the base of each sprout so they cook evenly.

5 In a large, heavy frying pan, melt the butter over medium heat. Stir in the chopped shallot and cook for 1–2 minutes until just softened, then add the Brussels sprouts and wine or water. Cook, covered, over medium heat for 6–8 minutes, shaking the pan and stirring occasionally, adding a little more water if necessary.

6 Add the poached chestnuts and toss gently to combine, then cover and cook for 3–5 minutes more, until the chestnuts and Brussels sprouts are tender.

Szechuan Aubergine

This medium-hot dish is also known as fish-fragrant aubergine in China, because the aubergine is cooked with flavourings that are often used with fish.

INGREDIENTS

Serves 4

2 small aubergines

5 ml/1 tsp salt

3 dried red chillies

peanut oil, for deep frying

3–4 garlic cloves, finely chopped

1 cm/½ in piece of fresh root ginger, finely chopped

4 spring onions, cut into 2.5 cm/1 in lengths (white and green parts separated)

15 ml/1 tbsp Chinese rice wine or medium-dry sherry

15 ml/1 tbsp light soy sauce

5 ml/1 tsp sugar

1.5 ml/¼ tsp ground roasted Szechuan peppercorns

15 ml/1 tbsp Chinese rice vinegar

5 ml/1 tsp sesame oil

1 Trim the aubergines and cut into strips about 4 cm/1½ in wide and 7.5 cm/3 in long. Place the aubergine strips in a colander and sprinkle over the salt. Set aside for 30 minutes, then rinse thoroughly under cold running water. Pat dry with kitchen paper.

2 Meanwhile, soak the chillies in warm water for 15 minutes. Drain, then cut each chilli into four pieces, discarding the seeds.

3 Half-fill a wok with oil and heat to 180°C/350°F. Deep-fry the aubergine until golden brown. Drain on kitchen paper. Pour off most of the oil from the wok. Reheat the oil and add the garlic, ginger and white spring onion.

4 Stir-fry for 30 seconds. Add the aubergine and toss, then add the rice wine or sherry, soy sauce, sugar, ground peppercorns and rice vinegar. Stir-fry for 1–2 minutes. Sprinkle over the sesame oil and green spring onion and serve immediately.

Chinese Greens with Soy Sauce

In this recipe, Chinese greens are prepared in a very simple way – stir-fried and served with soy sauce. The combination makes a very simple, quickly prepared, tasty accompaniment.

INGREDIENTS

Serves 3-4

450 g/1 lb Chinese greens
30 ml/2 tbsp peanut oil
15–30 ml/1–2 tbsp plum sauce

2 Heat a wok until hot, add the oil and swirl it around.

3 Add the Chinese greens and stir-fry for 2–3 minutes, until the greens have wilted a little.

4 Add the plum sauce and continue to stir-fry for a few seconds more, until the greens are cooked but still slightly crisp. Serve immediately.

1 Trim the Chinese greens, removing any discoloured leaves and damaged stems. Tear into manageable pieces.

VARIATION

You can replace the Chinese greens with Chinese flowering cabbage or Chinese broccoli, which is also known by its Cantonese name, choi sam. It has green leaves and tiny yellow flowers, which are also eaten along with the leaves and stalks. It is available at Asian markets.

Sweet and Sour Onions

Cooked in this way, sweet baby onions make an unusual yet tasty side dish. This recipe originated in the Provence region of France.

INGREDIENTS

Serves 6

450 g/1 lb baby onions, peeled

50 ml/2 fl oz/¼ cup wine vinegar

45 ml/3 tbsp olive oil

40 g/1½ oz/3 tbsp caster sugar

45 ml/3 tbsp tomato purée

1 bay leaf

2 sprigs of fresh parsley

65 g/2½ oz/½ cup raisins

salt and freshly ground black pepper

1 Put all the ingredients in a saucepan with 300 ml/ ½ pint/1¼ cups water. Bring to the boil and simmer gently, uncovered, for 45 minutes or until the onions are tender and most of the liquid has evaporated.

2 Remove the bay leaf and parsley, check the seasoning and transfer to a serving dish. Serve at room temperature.

Spinach with Raisins and Pine Nuts

Raisins and pine nuts are perfect partners. Here, tossed with wilted spinach and croûtons their contrasting textures make a delicious main meal accompaniment.

INGREDIENTS

Serves 4

50 g/2 oz/⅓ cup raisins

1 thick slice crusty white bread

45 ml/3 tbsp olive oil

25 g/1 oz/⅓ cup pine nuts

500 g/1¼ lb young spinach,
   stalks removed

2 garlic cloves, crushed

salt and freshly ground black pepper

1 Put the raisins in a small bowl with boiling water and leave to soak for 10 minutes. Drain.

2 Cut the bread into cubes and discard the crusts. Heat 30 ml/2 tbsp of the oil and fry the bread until golden. Drain.

3 Heat the remaining oil in the pan. Fry the pine nuts until they are beginning to colour. Add the spinach and garlic and cook quickly, turning the spinach until it has just wilted.

4 Toss in the raisins and season with salt and pepper. Transfer to a warmed serving dish. Scatter with croûtons and serve hot.

VARIATION

Use Swiss chard or spinach beet instead of the spinach, and cook them a little longer.

Hot Parsnip Fritters on Baby Spinach

Deep-frying brings out the luscious sweetness of parsnips, and their flavour is perfectly complemented by walnut-dressed baby spinach leaves.

INGREDIENTS

Serves 4

2 large parsnips

115 g/4 oz/1 cup plain flour

1 egg, separated

120 ml/4 fl oz/½ cup milk

115 g/4 oz baby spinach leaves, washed and dried

30 ml/2 tbsp olive oil

15 ml/1 tbsp walnut oil

15 ml/1 tbsp sherry vinegar

oil for deep frying

15 ml/1 tbsp coarsely chopped walnuts

salt, freshly ground black pepper and cayenne pepper

1 Peel the parsnips, bring to the boil in a pan of salted water and simmer for 10–15 minutes, until tender but not in the least mushy. Drain, cool and cut diagonally into slices about 5 cm/2 in long x 5 mm–1 cm/¼–½ in thick.

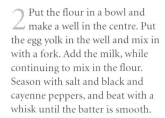

2 Put the flour in a bowl and make a well in the centre. Put the egg yolk in the well and mix in with a fork. Add the milk, while continuing to mix in the flour. Season with salt and black and cayenne peppers, and beat with a whisk until the batter is smooth.

3 Put the spinach leaves in a bowl. Mix the oils and vinegar. Season with salt and pepper.

4 When you are ready to serve, whisk the egg white to soft peaks, fold in a little of the yolk batter, then fold the white into the batter. Heat the oil for frying.

5 Shake the dressing vigorously, then toss the salad in the dressing. Arrange the leaves on 4 plates and scatter with walnuts.

6 Dip the parsnip slices in batter and fry until puffy and golden. Drain on kitchen paper and keep warm. Arrange the fritters on top of the salad leaves.

Parsnip and Chestnut Croquettes

The distinctive sweet nutty taste of chestnuts blends perfectly with the similarly sweet but earthy flavour of parsnips. Fresh chestnuts need to be peeled but frozen chestnuts are easy to use and are nearly as good as fresh for this recipe.

INGREDIENTS

Makes 10–12

450 g/1 lb parsnips, cut roughly into small
   pieces
115 g/4 oz frozen chestnuts
25 g/1 oz/2 tbsp butter
1 garlic clove, crushed
15 ml/1 tbsp chopped fresh coriander
1 egg, beaten
40–50 g/1½–2 oz fresh white breadcrumbs
vegetable oil, for frying
salt and freshly ground black pepper
sprig of fresh coriander, to garnish

1 Place the parsnips in a saucepan with enough water to cover. Bring to the boil, cover and simmer for 15–20 minutes.

2 Place the frozen chestnuts in a pan of water, bring to the boil and simmer for 8–10 minutes. Drain, place in a bowl and mash roughly into a pulp.

3 Melt the butter in a saucepan and cook the garlic for 30 seconds. Drain the parsnips and mash with the garlic butter. Stir in the chestnuts and coriander. Season with salt and pepper.

4 Take about 15 ml/1 tbsp of the mixture at a time and form into small croquettes, about 7.5 cm/3 in long. Dip each croquette into the beaten egg and then roll in the breadcrumbs.

5 Heat a little oil in a frying pan and fry each of the croquettes for 3–4 minutes until crisp and golden, turning frequently so they brown evenly.

6 Drain the croquettes on sheets of kitchen paper, wiping away any excess oil, and serve at once, garnished with sprigs of fresh coriander.

Balti Baby Vegetables

There is a wide and wonderful selection of baby vegetables available in supermarkets these days, and this simple recipe does full justice to their delicate flavour and attractive appearance. Serve as part of a main meal or even as a light appetizer.

INGREDIENTS

Serves 4–6

10 new potatoes, halved

12–14 baby carrots

12–14 baby courgettes

30 ml/2 tbsp corn oil

15 baby onions

30 ml/2 tbsp chilli sauce

5 ml/1 tsp garlic pulp

5 ml/1 tsp ginger pulp

5 ml/1 tsp salt

400 g/14 oz can chick-peas, drained

10 cherry tomatoes

5 ml/1 tsp crushed dried red chillies and
   30 ml/2 tbsp sesame seeds, to garnish

1 Bring a medium pan of salted water to the boil and add the new potatoes and baby carrots. After about 12–15 minutes, add the courgettes and boil for a further 5 minutes, or until all the vegetables are just tender.

2 Drain the vegetables well and set to one side.

3 Heat the oil in a deep round-bottomed frying pan or wok and add the baby onions. Fry until the onions turn golden brown. Lower the heat and add the chilli sauce, garlic, ginger and salt, taking care not to burn the mixture.

4 Add the chick-peas and stir-fry over medium heat until the moisture has been absorbed.

5 Add the cooked vegetables and cherry tomatoes and continue frying over medium heat, stirring with a slotted spoon for about 2 minutes.

6 Garnish with crushed red chillies and sesame seeds and serve.

VARIATION

By varying the vegetables chosen and experimenting with different combinations, this recipe can form the basis for a variety of delicious vegetable accompaniments. Try different vegetables, such as baby sweetcorn, French beans, mangetouts, okra, sugar snap peas and cauliflower florets, too.

Spring Vegetable Stir-fry

A colourful, dazzling medley of fresh and sweet young vegetables.

INGREDIENTS

Serves 4

15 ml/1 tbsp peanut oil

1 garlic clove, sliced

2.5 cm/1 in piece of fresh root ginger,
    finely chopped

115 g/4 oz baby carrots

115 g/4 oz patty pan squash

115 g/4 oz baby sweetcorn

115 g/4 oz French beans, topped
    and tailed

115 g/4 oz sugar snap peas, topped
    and tailed

115 g/4 oz young asparagus, cut into
    7.5 cm/3 in pieces

8 spring onions, trimmed and cut into
    5 cm/2 in pieces

115 g/4 oz cherry tomatoes

For the dressing

juice of 2 limes

15 ml/1 tbsp runny honey

15 ml/1 tbsp soy sauce

5 ml/1 tsp sesame oil

1 Heat the peanut oil in a wok or large frying pan.

2 Add the garlic and root ginger and stir-fry over high heat for 1 minute.

3 Add the carrots, patty pan squash, baby sweetcorn and beans and stir-fry for another 3–4 minutes.

4 Add the sugar snap peas, asparagus, spring onions and cherry tomatoes and stir-fry for a further 1–2 minutes.

5 Mix the dressing ingredients together and add to the pan.

6 Stir well and then cover the pan. Cook for 2–3 minutes more, until the vegetables are just tender but still crisp.

C O O K ' S   T I P

Stir-fries take only moments to cook, so prepare this dish at the last minute.

Fried Noodles, Beansprouts and Asparagus

Soft fried noodles contrast beautifully with crisp beansprouts and asparagus in this super-quick recipe.

INGREDIENTS

Serves 2

115 g/4 oz dried egg noodles

60 ml/4 tbsp vegetable oil

1 small onion, chopped

2.5 cm/1 in piece of fresh root ginger, peeled and grated

2 garlic cloves, crushed

175 g/6 oz young asparagus spears, trimmed

115 g/4 oz beansprouts

4 spring onions, sliced

45 ml/3 tbsp soy sauce

salt and freshly ground black pepper

1 Bring a pan of salted water to the boil. Add the noodles and cook for 2–3 minutes, until just tender. Drain and toss in 30 ml/2 tbsp of the oil.

2 Heat the remaining oil in a wok or frying pan until very hot. Add the onion, ginger and garlic and stir-fry for 2–3 minutes. Add the asparagus and stir-fry for 2–3 minutes more.

3 Add the egg noodles and beansprouts and stir-fry for 2 minutes.

4 Stir in the spring onions and soy sauce. Season with salt and pepper, adding salt sparingly as the soy sauce will probably supply enough salt in itself. Stir-fry for 1 minute then serve at once.

Deep-fried Root Vegetables with Spiced Salt

All kinds of root vegetables may be finely sliced and deep-fried to make 'chips'. Serve as an accompaniment to an oriental-style meal or simply by themselves as a nibble.

INGREDIENTS

Serves 4–6

1 carrot

2 parsnips

2 raw beetroot

1 sweet potato

peanut oil, for deep frying

1.5 ml/¼ tsp cayenne pepper

1 tsp sea salt flakes

1 Peel all the vegetables, then slice the carrot and parsnips into long, thin ribbons, and the beetroot and sweet potato into thin rounds. Pat dry all the vegetables on kitchen paper.

COOK'S TIP

To save time, you can slice the vegetables using a mandoline or a blender or food processor with a thin slicing disc attached.

2 Half-fill a wok with oil and heat to 180°C/350°F. Add the vegetable slices in batches and deep-fry for 2–3 minutes, until golden and crisp. Remove and drain on kitchen paper.

3 Place the cayenne pepper and sea salt in a mortar and grind together to a coarse powder.

4 Pile up the vegetable 'chips' on a serving plate and sprinkle over the spiced salt.

Vegetables Provençal

The flavours of the Mediterranean shine through in this delicious side dish.

INGREDIENTS

Serves 6

1 onion, sliced
2 leeks, sliced
2 garlic cloves, crushed
1 red pepper, seeded and sliced
1 green pepper, seeded and sliced
1 yellow pepper, seeded and sliced
350 g/12 oz courgettes, sliced
225 g/8 oz mushrooms, sliced
400 g/14 oz can chopped tomatoes
30 ml/2 tbsp ruby port
30 ml/2 tbsp tomato purée
15 ml/1 tbsp tomato ketchup
400 g/14 oz can chick-peas
115 g/4 oz/1 cup pitted black olives
45 ml/3 tbsp chopped fresh mixed herbs
salt and freshly ground black pepper
chopped fresh mixed herbs, to garnish

1 Put the onion, leeks, garlic, peppers, courgettes and mushrooms into a large saucepan.

2 Add the tomatoes, port, tomato purée and tomato ketchup and mix well.

3 Rinse and drain the chick-peas and add to the pan.

4 Cover, bring to the boil and simmer gently for 20–30 minutes, stirring occasionally, until the vegetables are cooked and tender but not overcooked.

5 Remove the lid and increase the heat slightly for the last 10 minutes of the cooking time, to thicken the sauce, if liked.

6 Stir in the olives and herbs and season with salt and pepper. Serve immediately, garnished with a scattering of chopped mixed herbs.

Spicy Chick-peas

Chick-peas are used and cooked in a variety of ways all over the Indian sub-continent. Tamarind gives this spicy dish a deliciously sharp, tangy flavour.

INGREDIENTS

Serves 4

225 g/8 oz/1¼ cups dried chick-peas

50 g/2 oz tamarind pulp

120 ml/4 fl oz/½ cup boiling water

45 ml/3 tbsp corn oil

2.5 ml/½ tsp cumin seeds

1 onion, finely chopped

2 garlic cloves, crushed

2.5 cm/1 in piece of fresh root ginger, peeled and grated

1 fresh green chilli, finely chopped

5 ml/1 tsp ground cumin

5 ml/1 tsp ground coriander

1.5 ml/¼ tsp ground turmeric

2.5 ml/½ tsp salt

225 g/8 oz tomatoes, skinned and finely chopped

2.5 ml/½ tsp garam masala

chopped fresh chillies and chopped onion, to garnish

1 Put the chick-peas in a large bowl and cover with plenty of cold water. Leave to soak overnight.

2 Drain the chick-peas and place in a large saucepan with double the volume of cold water. Bring to the boil and boil vigorously for 10 minutes. Skim off any scum. Cover and simmer for 1½–2 hours, or until the chick-peas are soft.

3 Meanwhile, break up the tamarind and soak in the boiling water for about 15 minutes. Rub the tamarind through a sieve into a bowl, discarding any stones and fibre.

COOK'S TIP

To save time, make double the quantity of tamarind pulp and freeze in ice-cube trays. It will keep for up to 2 months.

4 Heat the oil in a large saucepan and fry the cumin seeds for 2 minutes, until they splutter. Add the onion, garlic, ginger and chilli and fry for 5 minutes.

5 Add the cumin, coriander, turmeric and salt and fry for 3–4 minutes. Add the tomatoes and tamarind pulp. Bring to the boil and simmer for 5 minutes.

6 Add the chick-peas and garam masala. Cover and simmer for about 45 minutes. Garnish with chopped chillies and onion.

Frijoles

*A traditional Mexican bean dish
that tastes great with tortillas and
vegetable chilli.*

INGREDIENTS

Serves 6–8

350 g/12 oz/1¼–1½ cups dried red kidney,
   pinto or black haricot beans, picked
   over and rinsed
2 onions, finely chopped
2 garlic cloves, chopped
1 bay leaf
1 or more small fresh green chillies
30 ml/2 tbsp corn oil
2 tomatoes, peeled, seeded and chopped
salt
sprigs of fresh bay leaves, to garnish

1 Put the beans into a pan and
add cold water to cover
by 2.5 cm/1 in.

2 Add half the onion, half the
garlic, the bay leaf and the
chilli or chillies. Bring to the boil
and boil vigorously for about 10
minutes. Put the beans and liquid
into an earthenware pot or large
saucepan, cover and cook over low
heat for 30 minutes. Add boiling
water if the mixture starts to
become dry.

3 When the beans begin to
wrinkle, add 15 ml/1 tbsp of
the corn oil and cook for a further
30 minutes, or until the beans are
tender. Add salt to taste and cook
for 30 minutes more, but try to
avoid adding any more water.

4 Remove the beans from the
heat. Heat the remaining oil in
a small frying pan and sauté the
remaining onion and garlic
together until the onion is soft.
Add the tomatoes and cook for a
few minutes more.

5 Spoon 45 ml/3 tbsp of the
beans out of the pot or pan
and add them to the tomato
mixture. Mash to a paste. Stir into
the beans to thicken the liquid.
Cook for just long enough to heat
through, if necessary. Serve the
beans in small bowls and garnish
with fresh bay leaves.

Peas with Baby Onions and Cream

Ideally, use fresh peas and fresh baby onions. Frozen peas are an acceptable substitute if fresh ones aren't available, but frozen onions tend to be insipid and are not worth using. Alternatively, use the white parts of spring onions.

INGREDIENTS

Serves 4

175 g/6 oz baby onions

15 g/½ oz/1 tbsp butter

900 g/2 lb fresh peas (about 350 g/12 oz shelled or frozen)

150 ml/¼ pint/⅔ cup double cream

15 g/½ oz/2 tbsp plain flour

10 ml/2 tsp chopped fresh parsley

15–30 ml/1–2 tbsp lemon juice (optional)

salt and freshly ground black pepper

1 Peel the onions and halve them if necessary. Melt the butter in a flameproof casserole and fry the onions for 5–6 minutes over a moderate heat, until they begin to be flecked with brown.

2 Add the peas and stir-fry for a few minutes. Add 120 ml/ 4 fl oz/½ cup water and bring to the boil. Partially cover and simmer for about 10 minutes, until the peas and onions are tender. There should be a thin layer of water on the base of the pan – add a little more water if necessary or, if there is too much liquid, remove the lid and increase the heat until the liquid is reduced.

3 Using a small whisk, blend the cream with the flour. Remove the pan from the heat and stir in the combined cream and flour and chopped parsley. Season with salt and pepper.

4 Cook over a gentle heat for 3–4 minutes, until the sauce is thick. Taste and adjust the seasoning; add a little lemon juice to sharpen, if desired.

Red Cabbage in Port and Red Wine

A sweet and sour, spicy red cabbage dish, with the added crunch of pears and walnuts.

INGREDIENTS

Serves 6

15 ml/1 tbsp walnut oil

1 onion, sliced

2 whole star anise

5 ml/1 tsp ground cinnamon

pinch of ground cloves

450 g/1 lb red cabbage, finely shredded

25 g/1 oz/2 tbsp dark brown sugar

45 ml/3 tbsp red wine vinegar

300 ml/½ pint/1¼ cups red wine

150 ml/¼ pint/⅔ cup port

2 pears, cut into 1 cm/½ in cubes

115 g/4 oz/½ cup raisins

115 g/4 oz/½ cup walnut halves

salt and freshly ground black pepper

1 Heat the oil in a large pan. Add the onion and cook gently for about 5 minutes, until softened.

2 Add the star anise, cinnamon, cloves and cabbage and cook for about 3 minutes more.

COOK'S TIP

You can braise this dish in a low oven for up to 1½ hours.

3 Stir in the sugar, vinegar, red wine and port. Cover the pan and simmer gently for 10 minutes, stirring occasionally.

4 Stir in the cubed pears and raisins and cook for a further 10 minutes, or until the cabbage is tender. Season with salt and pepper. Mix in the walnut halves and serve.

Beetroot and Celeriac Gratin

Beautiful ruby-red slices of beetroot and celeriac make a stunning light accompaniment to any main course dish.

Serves 6

350 g/12 oz raw beetroot

350 g/12 oz raw celeriac

4 sprigs of fresh thyme, chopped

6 juniper berries, crushed

120 ml/4 fl oz/½ cup fresh orange juice

120 ml/4 fl oz/½ cup vegetable stock

salt and freshly ground black pepper

1 Preheat the oven to 190°C/375°F/Gas 5. Peel and slice the beetroot very finely. Quarter and peel the celeriac and slice very finely.

2 Fill a 25 cm/10 in diameter, cast iron, ovenproof or flame-proof frying pan with alternate layers of beetroot and celeriac slices, sprinkling with thyme, juniper and salt and pepper between each layer.

3 Mix the orange juice and stock together and pour over the gratin. Place over a medium heat and bring to the boil. Boil for 2 minutes.

4 Cover with foil and place in the oven for 15–20 minutes. Remove the foil and raise the oven temperature to 200°C/400°F/Gas 6. Cook for a further 10 minutes.

Runner Beans with Garlic

Delicate and fresh-tasting flageolet beans and sautéed garlic add a distinctly French flavour to this simple side dish.

INGREDIENTS

Serves 4

225 g/8 oz/1¼ cups flageolet beans
15 ml/1 tbsp olive oil
25 g/1 oz/2 tbsp butter
1 onion, finely chopped
1–2 garlic cloves, crushed
3–4 tomatoes, peeled and chopped
350 g/12 oz runner beans, prepared
    and sliced
150 ml/¼ pint/⅔ cup white wine
150 ml/¼ pint/⅔ cup vegetable stock
30 ml/2 tbsp chopped fresh parsley
salt and freshly ground black pepper

1 Place the flageolet beans in a large saucepan of water, bring to the boil and simmer for ¾–1 hour, until tender.

2 Heat the olive oil and butter in a large frying pan and sauté the onion and garlic for 3–4 minutes, until soft.

3 Add the chopped tomatoes to the onions in the pan and continue cooking over a gentle heat, until they are soft.

4 Stir the flageolet beans into the onion and tomato mixture, then add the runner beans, wine, stock and a little salt. Stir. Cover and simmer for 5–10 minutes.

5 Increase the heat to reduce the liquid, then stir in the parsley, more salt, if necessary, and pepper.

Green Lima Beans in Chilli Sauce

Try this fabulous dish of lima beans with a tomato and chilli sauce for warming up on winter evenings.

Serves 4

450 g/1 lb green lima or broad beans, thawed if frozen

30 ml/2 tbsp olive oil

1 onion, finely chopped

2 garlic cloves, chopped

350 g/12 oz tomatoes, peeled, seeded and chopped

1 or 2 drained canned jalapeño chillies, seeded and chopped

salt

chopped fresh coriander, to garnish

1 Cook the beans in a saucepan of boiling water for 15–20 minutes, until tender. Drain and keep hot, to one side, in the covered saucepan.

2 Heat the olive oil in a frying pan and sauté the onion and garlic until the onion is soft but not brown. Add the tomatoes and cook until the mixture thickens.

3 Add the jalapeños and cook for 1–2 minutes. Season with salt.

4 Pour the mixture over the reserved beans and check that they are hot. If not, return everything to the frying pan and cook over low heat for just long enough to heat through. Put into a warmed serving dish, garnish with coriander and serve.

Courgettes with Sun-dried Tomatoes

Sun-dried tomatoes have a concentrated, sweet flavour that goes well with courgettes.

INGREDIENTS

Serves 6

10 sun-dried tomatoes, dry or preserved
    in oil and drained
175 ml/6 fl oz/¾ cup warm water
75 ml/5 tbsp olive oil
1 large onion, finely sliced
2 garlic cloves, finely chopped
1 kg/2¼ lb courgettes, cut into thin strips
salt and freshly ground black pepper

1 Slice the sun-dried tomatoes into thin strips. Place in a bowl with the warm water. Allow to stand for 20 minutes.

2 In a large frying pan or saucepan, heat the oil and stir in the onion. Cook over low to moderate heat until the onion softens but does not brown.

3 Stir in the garlic and courgette strips. Cook for about 5 minutes, continuing to stir the mixture.

4 Stir in the tomatoes and their soaking liquid. Season with salt and pepper. Raise the heat slightly and cook until the courgettes are just tender. Adjust seasoning and serve hot or cold.

Tomato and Okra Stew

Okra is an unusual and delicious vegetable. It releases a sticky sap when cooked, which helps to thicken the stew.

INGREDIENTS

Serves 6

15 ml/1 tbsp olive oil
1 onion, chopped
350 g/12 oz jar pimientos, drained
2 x 400 g/14 oz cans chopped tomatoes
275 g/10 oz okra
30 ml/2 tbsp chopped fresh parsley
salt and freshly ground black pepper

1 Heat the oil in a heavy-based pan. Add the onion and cook for 2–3 minutes.

2 Coarsely chop the pimientos and add to the onion. Add the chopped tomatoes and mix well.

3 Cut the tops off the okra and cut into halves or quarters if large. Add to the tomato sauce in the pan. Season with plenty of salt and pepper.

4 Bring the vegetable stew to the boil. Then lower the heat, cover the pan and simmer for 12 minutes, until the vegetables are tender and the sauce has thickened. Stir in the chopped parsley and serve at once.

Glazed Carrots with Cider

This recipe is extremely simple to make. The carrots are cooked in the minimum of liquid to bring out the best of their flavour, and the cider adds a pleasant sharpness.

Serves 4

450 g/1 lb young carrots

25 g/1 oz/2 tbsp butter

15 ml/1 tbsp brown sugar

120 ml/4 fl oz/½ cup cider

60 ml/4 tbsp vegetable stock or water

1 tsp Dijon mustard

15 ml/1 tbsp finely chopped fresh parsley

1 Trim the tops and bottoms of the carrots. Peel or scrape them. Using a sharp knife, cut them into julienne strips.

COOK'S TIP

If the carrots are cooked before the liquid in the saucepan has reduced, transfer the carrots to a serving dish and rapidly boil the liquid until thick. Pour over the carrots and sprinkle with parsley.

2 Melt the butter in a frying pan, add the carrots and sauté for 4–5 minutes, stirring frequently. Sprinkle over the sugar and cook, stirring, for 1 minute or until the sugar has dissolved.

3 Add the cider and stock or water, bring to the boil and stir in the Dijon mustard. Partially cover the pan and simmer for 10–12 minutes, until the carrots are just tender. Remove the lid and continue cooking until the liquid has reduced to a thick sauce.

4 Remove the saucepan from the heat, stir in the chopped fresh parsley and then spoon into a warmed serving dish.

Broccoli and Cauliflower Gratin

*Broccoli and cauliflower make an
attractive combination, and a
yogurt and cheesy sauce gives them
extra piquant flavour.*

INGREDIENTS

Serves 4

1 small cauliflower (about 250 g/9 oz)

1 small head broccoli (about 250 g/9 oz)

150 g/5 oz/½ cup natural yogurt

75 g/3 oz/1 cup grated Cheddar cheese

5 ml/1 tsp wholegrain mustard

30 ml/2 tbsp wholemeal breadcrumbs

salt and freshly ground black pepper

1 Break the cauliflower and
broccoli into florets and cook
in lightly salted boiling water for
about 8–10 minutes, until just
tender. Drain well and transfer to
a flameproof dish.

COOK'S TIP

When preparing the cauliflower
and broccoli, discard the tougher
parts of the stalk, then break the
florets into even-size pieces so
they cook evenly.

2 Mix together the yogurt,
grated cheese and mustard,
then season the mixture with salt
and pepper and spoon over the
cauliflower and broccoli.

3 Preheat the grill to moderately
hot. Sprinkle the breadcrumbs
over the top of the vegetables and
grill until golden brown. Serve hot.

LIGHT
LUNCHES

~

Summer Tomato Pasta

This is a deliciously light pasta dish, full of fresh flavours. Use buffalo-milk mozzarella if you can – the flavour is noticeably better.

INGREDIENTS

Serves 4

275 g/10 oz/2¼ cups dried penne
450 g/1 lb plum tomatoes
275 g/10 oz mozzarella, drained
60 ml/4 tbsp olive oil
15 ml/1 tbsp balsamic vinegar
grated rind and juice of 1 lemon
15 fresh basil leaves, shredded
salt and freshly ground black pepper
fresh basil leaves, to garnish

3 Mix together the olive oil, balsamic vinegar, grated lemon rind, 15 ml/1 tbsp of the lemon juice and the basil. Season with salt and pepper. Add the tomatoes and mozzarella and leave to stand until the pasta is cooked.

4 Drain the pasta and toss with the tomato mixture. Serve immediately, garnished with fresh basil leaves.

1 Cook the pasta in boiling salted water, according to the package instructions, until just tender.

2 Quarter the tomatoes and remove the seeds, then chop the flesh into small cubes. Slice up the mozzarella into similarly sized pieces.

Pappardelle and Provençal Sauce

A classic French sauce of tomatoes and fresh vegetables adds colour and robust flavour to pasta.

INGREDIENTS

Serves 4

2 small purple onions, peeled, root left
   intact
150 ml/¼ pint/⅔ cup vegetable stock
1–2 garlic cloves, crushed
60 ml/4 tbsp red wine
2 courgettes, cut into fingers
1 yellow pepper, seeded and sliced
400 g/14 oz can tomatoes
10 ml/2 tsp chopped fresh thyme
5 ml/1 tsp caster sugar
350 g/12 oz pappardelle
salt and freshly ground black pepper
fresh thyme and 6 black olives, stoned and
   roughly chopped, to garnish

3 Cook the pasta in a large pan of boiling salted water according to the instructions on the package, until tender. Drain the pasta thoroughly.

4 Transfer to a warmed serving dish and top with the vegetables. Garnish with fresh thyme and chopped black olives.

1 Cut each onion into eight wedges through the root end, to hold them together during cooking. Put into a saucepan with the stock and garlic. Bring to the boil, cover and simmer for 5 minutes, until tender.

2 Add the red wine, courgettes, yellow pepper, tomatoes, thyme and sugar. Season with salt and pepper. Bring to the boil and cook gently for 5–7 minutes, shaking the pan occasionally to coat the vegetables with the sauce. (Do not overcook the vegetables as they are much nicer if they are slightly crunchy.)

Fusilli with Peppers and Onions

Grilling the peppers for this simple pasta dish intensifies their natural sweetness and gives them a delicious smoky flavour.

INGREDIENTS

Serves 4

450 g/1 lb red and yellow peppers (about 2 large ones)

90 ml/6 tbsp olive oil

1 large red onion, thinly sliced

2 cloves garlic, crushed

400 g/14 oz/4 cups fusilli or other short pasta

45 ml/3 tbsp finely chopped fresh parsley

salt and freshly ground black pepper

freshly grated Parmesan cheese, to serve

2 Peel the peppers. Cut them into quarters, remove the stems and seeds and slice the flesh into thin strips. Bring a large pan of water to the boil.

5 Meanwhile, add the peppers to the onions and mix together gently. Stir in about 45 ml/3 tbsp of the pasta cooking water. Season with salt and pepper. Stir in the chopped parsley.

1 Place the peppers under a hot grill and turn occasionally until they are black and blistered on all sides. Remove, place in a paper bag and leave for 5 minutes.

3 Heat the olive oil in a large frying pan. Add the onion and cook over moderate heat until it is translucent, 5–8 minutes. Stir in the garlic and cook for 2 minutes more.

6 Drain the pasta. Tip it into the pan with the vegetables and cook over moderate heat for 3–4 minutes, stirring constantly to mix the pasta into the sauce. Serve with the Parmesan passed separately.

4 Add salt and the pasta to the boiling water and cook until the pasta is tender.

COOK'S TIP

Peppers were brought to Europe by Christopher Columbus, who discovered them in Haiti. The large red, yellow and orange peppers are usually sweeter than the green varieties, and have a fuller flavour.

Pasta Primavera

There's no better way to showcase the best of the spring season's young vegetables than in this delightful pasta dish.

INGREDIENTS

Serves 4

225 g/8 oz thin asparagus spears, cut in half

115 g/4 oz mangetouts, topped and tailed

115 g/4 oz whole baby sweetcorn

225 g/8 oz whole baby carrots

1 small red pepper, seeded and chopped

8 spring onions, sliced

225 g/8 oz torchietti

150 ml/¼ pint/⅔ cup cottage cheese

150 ml/¼ pint/⅔ cup low-fat yogurt

15 ml/1 tbsp lemon juice

15 ml/1 tbsp chopped fresh parsley

milk (optional)

15 ml/1 tbsp snipped chives

salt and freshly ground black pepper

sun-dried tomato bread, to serve

3 Cook the pasta in a large pan of boiling salted water until tender. Drain thoroughly. Put the cottage cheese, yogurt, lemon juice and parsley into a food processor or blender. Season with salt and pepper, then process until smooth. Thin the sauce with a little milk, if necessary.

4 Put the sauce into a large pan with the pasta and vegetables, heat gently and toss carefully. Transfer to a warmed serving plate, scatter the chives over the top and serve with sun-dried tomato bread.

1 Cook the thin asparagus spears in a pan of boiling salted water for 3–4 minutes. Add the mangetouts halfway through the cooking time. Drain and rinse both under cold water.

2 Cook the baby sweetcorn, carrots, red pepper and spring onions in the same way until tender. Drain and rinse.

Penne with Fennel, Tomato and Blue Cheese

*The anise flavour of the fennel
makes it the perfect partner for
tomato, especially when topped with
blue cheese.*

INGREDIENTS

Serves 2

1 fennel bulb

225 g/8 oz/2 cups penne or other dried
   pasta shapes

30 ml/2 tbsp olive oil

1 shallot, finely chopped

300 ml/½ pint/1¼ cups passata

pinch of sugar

5 ml/1 tsp chopped fresh oregano

115 g/4 oz blue cheese

salt and freshly ground black pepper

1 Cut the fennel bulb in half. Cut
away the hard core and root.
Slice the fennel thinly, then cut the
slices into strips.

2 Bring a large pan of salted
water to the boil. Add the pasta
and cook for 10–12 minutes, until
just tender.

3 Meanwhile, heat the oil in a
small saucepan. Add the fennel
and shallot and cook for 2–3
minutes over high heat, stirring
occasionally.

4 Add the passata, sugar and
oregano. Cover the pan and
simmer gently for 10–12 minutes,
until the fennel is tender. Season
with salt and pepper. Drain the
pasta and return it to the pan. Toss
with the sauce. Serve with blue
cheese crumbled over the top.

Peanut Noodles

Add any of your favourite vegetables to this quick lunch recipe – and increase the quantity of chilli, if you can take the heat!

INGREDIENTS

Serves 4

200 g/7 oz medium egg noodles
30 ml/2 tbsp olive oil
2 garlic cloves, crushed
1 large onion, roughly chopped
1 red pepper, seeded and roughly chopped
1 yellow pepper, seeded and roughly chopped
350 g/12 oz courgettes, roughly chopped
150 g/5 oz/generous ¾ cup roasted unsalted peanuts, roughly chopped

For the dressing
50 ml/2 fl oz/¼ cup olive oil
grated rind and juice of 1 lemon
1 fresh red chilli, seeded and finely chopped
45 ml/3 tbsp snipped fresh chives
15–30 ml/1–2 tbsp balsamic vinegar
salt and freshly ground black pepper
snipped fresh chives, to garnish

1 Cook the noodles according to the package instructions and drain well.

2 Meanwhile, heat the oil in a very large frying pan or wok and cook the garlic and onion for 3 minutes, or until beginning to soften. Add the peppers and courgettes and cook for a further 15 minutes over a medium heat until beginning to soften and brown. Add the peanuts and cook for a further 1 minute.

3 Whisk together the olive oil, grated lemon rind and 45 ml/ 3 tbsp of the lemon juice, the chilli, chives and balsamic vinegar to taste. Season with salt and pepper.

4 Toss the noodles into the vegetables and stir-fry to heat through. Add the dressing, stir to coat and serve immediately, garnished with fresh chives.

Stir-fried Vegetables with Cashew Nuts

Stir-frying is the perfect way to make a delicious, colourful and very speedy meal.

INGREDIENTS

Serves 4

900 g/2 lb mixed vegetables (see Cook's Tip)

30–60 ml/2–4 tbsp sunflower or olive oil

2 garlic cloves, crushed

15 ml/1 tbsp grated fresh root ginger

50 g/2 oz/½ cup cashew nuts or 60 ml/ 4 tbsp sunflower seeds, pumpkin seeds or sesame seeds

soy sauce

salt and freshly ground black pepper

 1 Prepare the vegetables according to type. Carrots and cucumber should be cut into very fine matchsticks.

COOK'S TIP

Use a pack of stir-fry vegetables or make up your own mixture. Choose from carrots, mangetouts, baby sweetcorn, pak choi, cucumber, beansprouts, mushrooms, peppers and spring onions. Drained canned bamboo shoots and water chestnuts are delicious additions.

2 Heat a frying pan, then trickle the oil around the rim so that it runs down to coat the surface. When the oil is hot, add the garlic and ginger and cook for 2–3 minutes, stirring. Add the harder vegetables and toss over the heat for a further 5 minutes, until they start to soften.

3 Add the softer vegetables and stir-fry all of them over a high heat for 3–4 minutes.

4 Stir in the cashew nuts or seeds. Season with soy sauce, salt and pepper. Serve at once.

Rice Noodles with Vegetable Chilli Sauce

Fresh chilli and coriander combine to give this recipe quite a strong flavour kick.

INGREDIENTS

Serves 4

15 ml/1 tbsp sunflower oil

1 onion, chopped

2 garlic cloves, crushed

1 fresh red chilli, seeded and finely chopped

1 red pepper, seeded and diced

2 carrots, finely chopped

175 g/6 oz baby sweetcorn, halved

225 g/8 oz can sliced bamboo shoots, rinsed and drained

400 g/14 oz can red kidney beans, rinsed and drained

300 ml/½ pint/1¼ cups passata

15 ml/1 tbsp soy sauce

5 ml/1 tsp ground coriander

250 g/9 oz rice noodles

30 ml/2 tbsp chopped fresh coriander

salt and freshly ground black pepper

fresh parsley sprigs, to garnish

3 Meanwhile, place the noodles in a bowl and cover with boiling water. Stir with a fork and leave to stand for 3–4 minutes or according to the package instructions. Rinse and drain.

4 Stir the fresh coriander into the sauce. Spoon the noodles on to warmed serving plates, top with the sauce, garnish with parsley and serve.

1 Heat the oil in a saucepan, add the onion, garlic, chilli and red pepper and cook gently for 5 minutes, stirring. Add the carrots, sweetcorn, bamboo shoots, kidney beans, passata, soy sauce and ground coriander and stir to mix.

2 Bring to the boil, then cover and simmer gently for 30 minutes, stirring occasionally, until the vegetables are tender. Season with salt and pepper.

Frittata with Sun-dried Tomatoes

*Adding just a few sun-dried
tomatoes gives this frittata a
distinctly Mediterranean flavour.*

INGREDIENTS

Serves 3–4

6 sun-dried tomatoes, dry or in oil and
    drained
60 ml/4 tbsp olive oil
1 small onion, finely chopped
pinch of fresh thyme leaves
6 eggs
50 g/2 oz/½ cup freshly grated Parmesan
    cheese
salt and freshly ground black pepper

1 Place the tomatoes in a small
bowl and pour on enough hot
water to just cover them. Soak for
about 15 minutes. Lift the
tomatoes out of the water and slice
them into thin strips. Reserve the
soaking water.

2 Heat the oil in a large non-
stick or heavy frying pan. Stir
in the onion and cook for 5–6
minutes or until soft and golden.
Add the tomatoes and thyme and
continue to stir over moderate
heat for 2–3 minutes. Season with
salt and pepper.

3 Break the eggs into a bowl and
beat lightly with a fork. Stir in
45–60 ml/3–4 tbsp of the tomato
soaking water and the grated
Parmesan cheese.

4 Raise the heat under the pan.
When the oil is sizzling, pour
in the eggs. Mix them quickly into
the other ingredients and stop
stirring. Lower the heat to
moderate and cook for 4–5
minutes on the first side, or until
the frittata is puffed and golden
brown underneath.

5 Take a large plate, place it
upside down over the pan and,
holding it firmly with oven gloves,
turn the pan and the frittata over
on to it. Slide the frittata back into
the pan and continue cooking
until golden brown on the second
side, 3–4 minutes more. Remove
from the heat. The frittata can be
served hot, at room temperature or
cold. Cut it into wedges to serve.

Potato Gnocchi

Gnocchi are little dumplings made either with mashed potato and flour, as here, or with semolina. They should be light in texture, and must not be overworked while being made.

INGREDIENTS

Serves 4–6

1 kg/2¼ lb waxy potatoes, scrubbed

15 ml/1 tbsp salt

250–300 g/9–11 oz/2–2½ cups flour

1 egg

pinch of grated nutmeg

25 g/1 oz/2 tbsp butter

freshly grated Parmesan cheese, to serve

1 Place the unpeeled potatoes in a large pan of salted water. Bring to the boil and cook until the potatoes are tender but not falling apart. Drain. Peel as soon as possible, while the potatoes are still hot but cool enough to handle.

VARIATION

Green gnocchi are made in exactly the same way as potato gnocchi, with the addition of fresh or frozen spinach. Use 675 g/1½ lb fresh spinach, or 400 g/14 oz frozen leaf spinach. Mix with the potato and the flour in Step 2.

Almost any pasta sauce is suitable for serving with gnocchi; they are particularly good with a creamy Gorgonzola sauce, or simply drizzled with olive oil. Gnocchi can also be served in clear soup.

2 On a work surface, spread out a layer of flour. Mash the hot potatoes with a food mill, dropping them directly on to the flour. Sprinkle with about half of the remaining flour and mix very lightly into the potatoes.

3 Break the egg into the mixture, add the nutmeg and knead lightly, drawing in more flour as necessary. When the dough is light to the touch and no longer moist or sticky it is ready to be rolled. Do not overwork or the gnocchi will be heavy.

4 Divide the dough into 4 parts. On a lightly floured board form each part into a roll about 2 cm/¾ in in diameter, taking care not to overhandle the dough. Cut the rolls crosswise into pieces about 2 cm/¾ in long.

5 Hold an ordinary table fork with long tines sideways, leaning on the board. One by one, press and roll the gnocchi lightly along the tines of the fork towards the points, making ridges on one side and a depression from your thumb on the other.

6 Bring a large pan of water to a fast boil. Add salt and drop in about half the gnocchi.

7 When the gnocchi rise to the surface, after 3–4 minutes, the gnocchi are done. Scoop them out, allow to drain and place in a warmed serving bowl. Dot with butter. Keep warm while the remaining gnocchi are boiling. As soon as they are cooked, toss the gnocchi with the butter or a heated sauce, sprinkle with grated Parmesan and serve.

Vegetable Fajita

*A colourful medley of mushrooms
and peppers in a spicy sauce,
wrapped in tortillas and served with
creamy guacamole.*

INGREDIENTS

Serves 2

1 onion
1 red pepper
1 green pepper
1 yellow pepper
1 garlic clove, crushed
225 g/8 oz mushrooms
90 ml/6 tbsp vegetable oil
30 ml/2 tbsp medium chilli powder
salt and freshly ground black pepper

For the guacamole
1 ripe avocado
1 shallot, coarsely chopped
1 fresh green chilli, seeded and
    coarsely chopped
juice of 1 lime

To serve
4–6 flour tortillas, warmed
1 lime, cut into wedges
sprigs of fresh coriander

1 Slice the onion. Cut the
peppers in half, remove the
seeds and cut the flesh into strips.
Combine the onion and peppers in
a bowl. Add the crushed garlic and
mix lightly.

2 Remove the mushroom stalks.
Save for making stock, or
discard. Slice the mushroom caps
and add to the pepper mixture in
the bowl. Mix the oil and chilli
powder in a cup, pour over the
vegetable mixture and stir well.
Set aside.

3 Make the guacamole. Cut the
avocado in half and remove
the stone and the peel. Put the
flesh into a food processor or
blender with the shallot, green
chilli and lime juice.

4 Process for 1 minute, until
smooth. Scrape into a small
bowl, cover tightly and put in the
fridge to chill until required.

5 Heat a frying pan or wok until
very hot. Add the marinated
vegetables and stir-fry over high
heat for 5–6 minutes, until the
mushrooms and peppers are just
tender. Season with salt and
pepper. Spoon the filling on to
each tortilla and roll up. Garnish
with coriander and serve with the
guacamole and lime wedges.

Baked Eggs with Creamy Leeks

This is a traditional French way of enjoying eggs. You can vary the dish quite easily by experimenting with other vegetables, such as puréed spinach or ratatouille, as a base.

INGREDIENTS

Serves 4

15 g/½ oz/1 tbsp butter, plus extra
   for greasing
225 g/8 oz small leeks, thinly sliced
75–90 ml/5–6 tbsp whipping cream
freshly grated nutmeg
4 eggs
salt and freshly ground black pepper

1 Preheat the oven to 190°C/375°F/Gas 5. Generously butter the base and sides of four ramekin dishes or individual soufflé dishes.

2 Melt the butter in a small frying pan and cook the leeks over medium heat, stirring frequently, until softened but not browned.

VARIATION

Put 15 ml/1 tbsp of cream in each dish with some chopped herbs. Break in the eggs, add 15 ml/1 tbsp cream and a little grated cheese, then bake.

3 Add 45 ml/3 tbsp of the cream and cook gently for about 5 minutes, until the leeks are very soft and the cream has thickened a little. Season with salt, pepper and nutmeg.

4 Arrange the ramekins in a small roasting tin and divide the leeks among them. Break an egg into each, spoon 5–10 ml/1–2 tsp of the remaining cream over each egg and season lightly.

5 Pour boiling water into the roasting tin to come halfway up the side of the ramekins or soufflé dishes. Bake for about 10 minutes, until the whites are set and the yolks are still soft, or a little longer if you prefer them more well done.

Chinese Garlic Mushrooms

Tofu is high in protein and very low in fat, so it is a very useful food to keep handy for quick meals and snacks like this one.

INGREDIENTS

Serves 4

8 large open-cap mushrooms

3 spring onions, sliced

1 garlic clove, crushed

30 ml/2 tbsp mushroom sauce

275 g/10 oz packet marinated tofu
   (beancurd), cut into small dice

200 g/7 oz can sweetcorn, drained

10 ml/2 tsp sesame oil

salt and freshly ground black pepper

1 Preheat the oven to 200°C/400°F/Gas 6. Finely chop the mushroom stalks and mix with the spring onions, garlic and mushroom sauce.

2 Stir in the diced marinated tofu and sweetcorn, season with salt and pepper, then spoon the filling into the mushrooms.

3 Brush the edges of the mushrooms with the sesame oil. Arrange the stuffed mushrooms in a baking dish and bake for 12–15 minutes, until the mushrooms are just tender, then serve at once.

COOK'S TIP

If you prefer, omit the mushroom sauce and use light soy sauce instead.

Savoury Nut Loaf

This delicious nut loaf makes perfect picnic food.

Serves 4

15 ml/1 tbsp olive oil, plus extra for
  greasing
1 onion, chopped
1 leek, chopped
2 celery sticks, finely chopped
225 g/8 oz mushrooms, chopped
2 garlic cloves, crushed
425 g/15 oz can lentils, rinsed and drained
115 g/4 oz/1 cup mixed nuts, such as
  hazelnuts, cashew nuts and almonds,
  finely chopped
50 g/2 oz/½ cup flour
50 g/2 oz/½ cup grated mature Cheddar
  cheese
1 medium egg, beaten
45–60 ml/3–4 tbsp chopped fresh
  mixed herbs
salt and freshly ground black pepper
chives and sprigs of fresh flat leaf parsley,
  to garnish

1 Preheat the oven to
190°C/375°F/Gas 5. Lightly
grease the base and sides of a
900 g/2 lb loaf tin and line with
greaseproof paper.

2 Heat the oil in a large
saucepan, add the chopped
onion, leek, celery sticks and
mushrooms and the crushed
garlic, then cook gently for 10
minutes, until the vegetables have
softened, stirring occasionally.

3 Add the lentils, mixed nuts,
flour, grated cheese, egg and
herbs. Season with salt and pepper
and mix thoroughly.

4 Spoon the nut, vegetable and
lentil mixture into the
prepared loaf tin, ensuring that it
is pressed into the corners, and
level the surface. Bake, uncovered,
for 50–60 minutes, or until the nut
loaf is lightly browned on top and
firm to the touch.

5 Cool the loaf slightly in the
tin, then turn out on to a
serving plate. Serve hot or cold, cut
into slices and garnished with
chives and flat leaf parsley.

Spicy Bean and Lentil Loaf

An appetizing, high-fibre savoury
loaf, ideal for packed lunches.

INGREDIENTS

Serves 12

10 ml/2 tsp olive oil

1 onion, finely chopped

1 garlic clove, crushed

2 celery sticks, finely chopped

400 g/14 oz can red kidney beans

400 g/14 oz can lentils

1 egg

1 carrot, coarsely grated

50 g/2 oz/½ cup finely grated mature
    Cheddar cheese

50 g/2 oz/1 cup fresh wholemeal
    breadcrumbs

15 ml/1 tbsp tomato purée

15 ml/1 tbsp tomato ketchup

5 ml/1 tsp each ground cumin, ground
    coriander and hot chilli powder

salt and freshly ground black pepper

salad, to serve

1 Preheat the oven to
180°C/350°F/Gas 4. Lightly
grease a 900 g/2 lb loaf tin.

2 Heat the oil in a saucepan, add
the onion, garlic and celery and
cook gently for 5 minutes, stirring
occasionally. Remove the pan from
the heat and cool slightly.

3 Rinse and drain the beans and
lentils. Put in a blender or food
processor with the onion mixture
and egg and process until smooth.

4 Transfer the mixture to a bowl,
add all the remaining ingredients and mix well. Season with salt
and pepper.

5 Spoon the mixture into the
prepared tin and level the
surface. Bake for about 1 hour,
then remove from the tin and serve
hot or cold in slices, accompanied
by a salad.

Stuffed Mushrooms

*This is a classic mushroom dish,
strongly flavoured with garlic. Use
flat mushrooms or field mushrooms
that are sometimes available from
farm shops.*

Serves 4

450 g/1 lb large flat mushrooms

butter, for greasing

about 75 ml/5 tbsp olive oil

2 garlic cloves, crushed

45 ml/3 tbsp finely chopped fresh parsley

40–50 g/1½–2 oz/¾–1 cup fresh white
    breadcrumbs

salt and freshly ground black pepper

sprig of fresh flat leaf parsley, to garnish

1 Preheat the oven to
180°C/350°F/Gas 4. Cut off the
mushroom stalks and reserve.

2 Arrange the mushroom caps in
a buttered shallow dish, gill
side upwards.

3 Heat 15 ml/1 tbsp of the oil in
a frying pan and fry the garlic
briefly. Finely chop the mushroom
stalks and mix with the parsley and
breadcrumbs. Add the garlic and
15 ml/1 tbsp of the oil. Season with
salt and pepper. Pile a little of the
mixture into each mushroom.

4 Add the remaining oil to the
dish and cover the mushrooms
with buttered greaseproof paper.
Bake for 15–20 minutes, removing
the paper for the last five minutes
to brown the tops. Garnish with a
sprig of flat leaf parsley.

Baked Onions Stuffed with Feta

Serve these cheesy, nutty onions with warm olive bread for a fabulous lunch.

INGREDIENTS

Serves 4

4 large red onions

15 ml/1 tbsp olive oil

25 g/1 oz pine nuts

115 g/4 oz feta cheese, crumbled

25 g/1 oz/½ cup fresh white breadcrumbs

15 ml/1 tbsp chopped fresh coriander

salt and freshly ground black pepper

1 Preheat the oven to 180°C/350°F/Gas 4. Lightly grease a shallow ovenproof dish. Peel the onions and cut a thin slice from the top and base of each. Place the onions in a large saucepan of boiling water and cook for 10–12 minutes.

2 Remove the onions with a slotted spoon. Lay them out to drain on a sheet of kitchen paper and leave to cool slightly.

3 Using a small knife or your fingers, remove the inner sections of the onions, leaving about two or three outer rings. Finely chop the inner sections and place the outer shells in an ovenproof dish.

4 Heat the oil in a medium-size frying pan and fry the chopped onions for 4–5 minutes, until golden, then add the pine nuts and stir-fry for a few minutes.

5 Place the feta cheese in a small bowl and stir in the onions, pine nuts, breadcrumbs and coriander. Season with a little salt and pepper.

6 Spoon the mixture into the onion shells. Cover loosely with foil and bake for about 30 minutes, removing the foil for the last 10 minutes to allow them to brown slightly. Serve hot.

Onion Tarts with Goat's Cheese

A variation of a classic French dish, Tarte à l'Oignon, this recipe uses young goat's cheese as well as cream. The young goat's cheese is mild and creamy and complements the flavour of the onions.

INGREDIENTS

Serves 8

175 g/6 oz/1½ cups plain flour

65 g/2½ oz/5 tbsp butter

25 g/1 oz goat's cheese or Cheddar cheese, grated

For the filling

15–25 ml/1–1½ tbsp olive or sunflower oil

3 onions, finely sliced

175 g/6 oz young goat's cheese

2 eggs, beaten

15 ml/1 tbsp single cream

50 g/2 oz goat's cheddar, grated

15 ml/1 tbsp chopped fresh tarragon

salt and freshly ground black pepper

1 To make the pastry, sift the flour into a bowl and rub in the butter until the mixture resembles fine breadcrumbs. Stir in the cheese and enough cold water to make a dough. Knead lightly, put in a polythene bag and chill. Preheat the oven to 190°C/375°F/Gas 5.

2 Roll out the dough on a lightly floured surface, then cut into eight rounds using an 12 cm/4½ in pastry cutter, and line eight 10 cm/4 in bun tins. Prick the bases with a fork and bake in the oven for 10–15 minutes. Reduce the heat to 180°C/350°F/Gas 4.

3 Heat the oil in a large frying pan and fry the onions over a low heat for 20–25 minutes, until they are a deep golden brown. Stir to prevent them from burning.

4 Beat the goat's cheese with the eggs, cream, goat's cheddar and tarragon. Season with salt and pepper and then stir in the fried onions.

5 Pour the mixture into the part-baked pastry cases and bake in the oven for 20–25 minutes, until golden. Serve warm or cold with a green salad.

Sweetcorn and Cheese Pasties

These tasty pasties are really simple to make and extremely moreish. Why not make double – they'll go like hot cakes.

INGREDIENTS

Makes 18–20

250 g/9 oz sweetcorn

115 g/4 oz feta cheese

1 egg, beaten

30 ml/2 tbsp whipping cream

15 g/½ oz freshly grated Parmesan cheese

3 spring onions, chopped

8-10 small sheets filo pastry

115 g/4 oz/8 tbsp butter, melted

freshly ground black pepper

1 Preheat the oven to 190°C/375°F/Gas 5. Butter two bun tins.

2 If using fresh sweetcorn, strip the kernels from the cob using a large sharp knife, cutting downwards from top to bottom of the cob. Simmer in a little salted water for 3–5 minutes, until tender. For canned sweetcorn, drain and rinse well under cold running water.

3 Crumble the feta cheese into a bowl and stir in the sweetcorn. Add the egg, cream, Parmesan cheese, spring onions and ground black pepper and stir well.

4 Take one sheet of pastry and cut it in half to make a square. (Keep the remaining pastry covered with a damp cloth to prevent it from drying out.) Brush with melted butter and then fold into four to make a smaller square (about 7.5 cm/3 in).

5 Place a heaped teaspoon of mixture in the centre of each pastry square and then squeeze the pastry around the filling to make a 'money bag' casing.

6 Continue making pasties until all the filling is used up. Brush the outside of each 'bag' with any remaining butter and then bake for about 15 minutes, until golden brown. Serve hot.

Cheese and Spinach Flan

This flan freezes well and can be reheated. It makes an excellent addition to a festive buffet party.

INGREDIENTS

Serves 8

115 g/4 oz/8 tbsp butter
225 g/8 oz/2 cups plain flour
2.5 ml/½ tsp English mustard powder
2.5 ml/½ tsp paprika
large pinch of salt
115 g/4 oz Cheddar cheese, finely grated
1 egg, beaten, to glaze

For the filling

450 g/1 lb frozen spinach
1 onion, chopped
pinch of grated nutmeg
225 g/8 oz/1 cup cottage cheese
2 large eggs, beaten
50 g/2 oz freshly grated Parmesan cheese
150 ml/¼ pint/⅔ cup single cream
salt and freshly ground black pepper

1 Rub the butter into the flour until it resembles fine breadcrumbs. Stir in the mustard powder, paprika, salt and cheese. Bind to a dough with 45–60 ml/ 3–4 tbsp cold water. Knead until smooth, wrap and chill in the fridge for 30 minutes.

2 Put the spinach and onion in a pan, cover and cook slowly. Season with salt, pepper and nutmeg. Turn the spinach into a bowl and cool slightly. Add the remaining filling ingredients.

3 Roll out two-thirds of the pastry on a lightly floured surface and use it to line a 23 cm/ 9 in loose-based flan tin. Press it well into the edges, removing excess pastry with a rolling pin. Spoon the filling into the flan case.

4 Preheat the oven to 200°C/ 400°F/Gas 6. Put a baking tray in the oven to preheat.

5 Roll out the remaining pastry and cut it with a lattice pastry cutter. With the help of a rolling pin, lay it over the flan. Brush the joins with egg glaze. Press the edges together and trim off the excess pastry. Brush the pastry lattice with egg glaze and bake on the hot baking tray for 35–40 minutes, or until golden brown. Serve hot or cold.

Gado Gado

The peanut sauce on this traditional Indonesian vegetable dish owes its flavour to galangal, an aromatic rhizome that resembles ginger.

INGREDIENTS

Serves 4

250 g/9 oz white cabbage, shredded
4 carrots, cut into matchsticks
4 celery sticks, cut into matchsticks
250 g/9 oz/4 cups beansprouts
½ cucumber, cut into matchsticks
fried onion, salted peanuts and sliced
 fresh chilli, to garnish

For the peanut sauce
15 ml/1 tbsp oil
1 small onion, finely chopped
1 garlic clove, crushed
1 small piece galangal, peeled and grated
5 ml/1 tsp ground cumin
1.5 ml/¼ tsp ground chilli powder
5 ml/1 tsp tamarind paste or lime juice
60 ml/4 tbsp crunchy peanut butter
5 ml/1 tsp soft light brown sugar

1 Steam the cabbage, carrots and celery for about 3–4 minutes, until just tender. Leave to cool. Spread out the beansprouts on a large serving dish. Arrange the cabbage, carrots, celery and cucumber on top.

2 To make the sauce, heat the oil in a saucepan, add the onion and garlic and cook gently for 5 minutes, until soft.

COOK'S TIP

As long as the sauce remains the same, the vegetables can be altered at the whim of the cook and to reflect the contents of the vegetable rack or chiller.

3 Stir in the spices and cook for 1 minute more. Add the tamarind paste or lime juice, peanut butter and sugar. Mix well.

4 Heat the sauce gently, stirring occasionally and adding a little hot water if necessary, to make the sauce runny enough to coat the vegetables when poured.

5 Spoon a little of the sauce over the vegetables and toss lightly together. Garnish with fried onions, peanuts and sliced chilli. Serve the rest of the sauce in a bowl separately.

Sliced Frittata with Tomato Sauce

This dish – cold frittata with a tomato sauce – is ideal for a light summer lunch.

Serves 3–4

6 eggs

30 ml/2 tbsp finely chopped fresh mixed
   herbs, such as basil, parsley, thyme
   and tarragon

40 g/1½ oz/¼ cup freshly grated
   Parmesan cheese

45 ml/3 tbsp olive oil

salt and freshly ground black pepper

For the tomato sauce

30 ml/2 tbsp olive oil

1 small onion, finely chopped

350 g/12 oz fresh tomatoes, chopped, or
   400 g/14 oz can chopped tomatoes

1 garlic clove, chopped

salt and freshly ground black pepper

1 To make the frittata, break the eggs into a bowl and beat them lightly with a fork. Beat in the herbs and Parmesan. Season with salt and pepper. Heat the oil in a large non-stick or heavy frying pan until hot but not smoking.

2 Pour in the seasoned egg mixture. Cook, without stirring, until the frittata is puffed and golden brown underneath.

3 Take a large plate, place it upside down over the pan and, holding it firmly with oven gloves, turn the pan and the frittata over on to it. Slide the frittata back into the pan and continue cooking for about 3–4 minutes more until it is golden brown on the second side. Remove from the heat and allow to cool completely.

4 To make the tomato sauce, heat the oil in a medium-heavy saucepan. Add the onion and cook slowly until it is soft. Add the tomatoes, garlic and 60 ml/4 tbsp water and season with salt and pepper. Cover the pan and cook over moderate heat for about 15 minutes.

5 Remove from the heat and cool slightly before pressing the sauce through a food mill or sieve. Leave to cool completely.

6 To assemble the salad, cut the frittata into thin slices. Place them in a serving bowl and toss lightly with the sauce. Serve at room temperature or chilled.

Ratatouille

A classic vegetable stew, packed full of fresh vegetables and herbs and absolutely bursting with wonderful flavour.

Serves 4

2 large aubergines, roughly chopped

4 courgettes, roughly chopped

150 ml/¼ pint/⅔ cup olive oil

2 onions, sliced

2 garlic cloves, chopped

1 large red pepper, seeded and roughly chopped

2 large yellow peppers, seeded and roughly chopped

sprig of fresh rosemary

sprig of fresh thyme

5 ml/1 tsp coriander seeds, crushed

3 plum tomatoes, skinned, seeded and chopped

8 basil leaves, torn

salt and freshly ground black pepper

sprigs of fresh parsley or basil, to garnish

1 Sprinkle the aubergines and courgettes with salt, then put them in a colander with a plate and a weight on top to extract the bitter juices. Leave for about 30 minutes.

2 Heat the olive oil in a large saucepan. Add the onions and fry gently for 6–7 minutes, until just softened. Add the garlic and cook for another 2 minutes.

3 Rinse the aubergines and courgettes and pat dry with a clean dish towel. Add to the pan with the peppers, increase the heat and sauté until the peppers are just turning brown.

4 Add the herbs and coriander seeds, then cover the pan and cook gently for about 40 minutes.

5 Add the tomatoes and season with salt and pepper. Cook gently for a further 10 minutes, until the vegetables are soft but not too mushy. Remove the sprigs of herbs. Stir in the torn basil leaves and check the seasoning. Leave to cool slightly and serve warm or cold, garnished with sprigs of parsley or basil.

Sweetcorn Cakes with Grilled Tomatoes

Crisp sweetcorn fritters are simple to make and guaranteed to become a mid-day favourite.

INGREDIENTS

Serves 4

1 large cob sweetcorn

75 g/3 oz/³⁄₄ cup plain flour

1 egg

a little milk

2 large firm tomatoes

1 garlic clove, crushed

5 ml/1 tsp dried oregano

30–45 ml/2–3 tbsp olive oil, plus extra for shallow-frying

salt and freshly ground black pepper

8 cupped leaves iceberg lettuce, to serve

shredded fresh basil leaves, to garnish

1 Pull the husks and silk away from the corn, then hold the cob upright on a board and cut downwards with a heavy knife to strip off the kernels. Put the kernels in a pan of boiling water and cook for 3 minutes after the water has returned to the boil, then drain and rinse under the cold tap to cool quickly.

2 Put the flour into a bowl and break the egg into a well in the middle. Start stirring with a fork, adding a little milk to make a soft dropping consistency. Stir in the drained corn and season with salt and pepper.

3 Preheat the grill. Halve the tomatoes horizontally and make two or three criss-cross slashes across the cut side of each half. Rub in the crushed garlic and the oregano and season with salt and pepper. Trickle with oil and grill until lightly browned.

4 While the tomatoes grill, heat some oil in a wide frying pan and drop a tablespoon of batter into the centre. Cook, one at a time, over a low heat and turn as soon as the top is set. Drain on kitchen paper and keep warm while cooking the remaining fritters. The mixture should make at least 8 sweetcorn cakes.

5 For each serving, put 2 sweetcorn cakes on to lettuce leaves, garnish with basil and serve with a grilled tomato half.

Fresh Ceps with a Parsley Dressing

To capture the just-picked flavour of mushrooms, try this delicious salad enriched with an egg yolk and walnut oil dressing. Choose small ceps or bay boletus for a firm texture and a fine flavour.

INGREDIENTS

Serves 4

350 g/12 oz fresh ceps or bay boletus

175 g/6 oz mixed salad leaves such as bativia, young spinach and frisée

50 g/2 oz/½ cup broken walnut pieces, toasted

50 g/2 oz Parmesan cheese

salt and freshly ground black pepper

For the dressing

2 egg yolks

2.5 ml/½ tsp French mustard

75 ml/5 tbsp groundnut oil

45 ml/3 tbsp walnut oil

30 ml/2 tbsp lemon juice

30 ml/2 tbsp chopped fresh parsley

pinch of caster sugar

1 For the dressing, place the egg yolks in a screw-top jar with the mustard, oils, lemon juice, parsley and sugar. Shake well.

2 Slice the mushrooms thinly using a sharp knife.

3 Place the mushrooms in a large salad bowl and combine with the dressing. Leave to stand for 10–15 minutes for the flavours to mingle.

4 Wash and spin the salad leaves, then toss with the mushrooms.

5 Turn out on to four large plates, season with salt and pepper then scatter with toasted walnut pieces and shavings of Parmesan cheese.

COOK'S TIP

The dressing for this salad uses raw egg yolks. Be sure to use only the freshest eggs from a reputable supplier. Pregnant women, young children and the elderly are not advised to eat raw egg yolks. If this presents a problem, the dressing can be made without the egg yolks.

Sun-dried Tomato and Parmesan Carbonara

Ingredients for this recipe can easily be doubled up to serve four. Why not try it with plenty of garlic bread and a big green salad?

INGREDIENTS

Serves 2

175 g/6 oz tagliatelle

50 g/2 oz sun-dried tomatoes in olive
   oil, drained

2 eggs, beaten

150 ml/¼ pint/⅔ cup double cream

15 ml/1 tbsp wholegrain mustard

50 g/2 oz/⅔ cup Parmesan cheese,
   freshly grated

12 fresh basil leaves, shredded

salt and pepper

fresh basil leaves, to garnish

crusty bread, to serve

1 Cook the pasta in boiling, salted water until it is just tender but still retains a little bite (*al dente*).

2 Meanwhile, cut the sun-dried tomatoes into small pieces.

3 Beat together the eggs, cream and mustard in a bowl. Add plenty of salt and pepper until they are well combined and smooth but do not allow the mixture to become frothy.

4 Drain the pasta and immediately return to the hot saucepan with the cream mixture, sun-dried tomatoes, Parmesan cheese and shredded fresh basil. Return to a very low heat for 1 minute, stirring gently until the mixture thickens slightly. Adjust the seasoning and serve immediately, garnished with basil leaves. Serve with plenty of crusty bread.

Omelette with Beans

Every good cook should have a few omelettes in their repertoire. This version includes soft white beans and is finished with a layer of toasted sesame seeds.

INGREDIENTS

Serves 4

30 ml/2 tbsp olive oil

5 ml/1 tsp sesame oil

1 Spanish onion, chopped

1 small red pepper, seeded and diced

2 celery sticks, chopped

1 x 400 g/14 oz can soft white beans, drained

8 eggs

45 ml/3 tbsp sesame seeds

salt and freshly ground black pepper

green salad, to serve

3 In a small bowl, beat the eggs with a fork, season with salt and pepper and pour over the ingredients in the pan.

4 Stir the egg mixture with a flat wooden spoon until it begins to stiffen, then allow to firm over a low heat for 6-8 minutes.

5 Preheat a moderate grill. Sprinkle the omelette with sesame seeds and brown evenly under the grill.

6 Cut the omelette into thick wedges and serve warm with a green salad.

1 Heat the olive and sesame oils in a 30 cm/12 in flameproof frying pan. Add the onion, pepper and celery and cook to soften without colouring.

2 Add the beans and continue to cook for several minutes to heat through.

VARIATION

You can also use sliced cooked potatoes, any seasonal vegetables, baby artichoke hearts and chick-peas in this omelette.

Mushroom Picker's Omelette

Perfect for Sunday brunch, this omelette is simplicity itself to make.

INGREDIENTS

Serves 1

25 g/1 oz/2 tbsp unsalted butter, plus extra
   for cooking
115 g/4 oz assorted wild and cultivated
   mushrooms such as young ceps, bay
   boletus, chanterelles, saffron milk-caps,
   closed field mushrooms, oyster
   mushrooms, hedgehog and St George's
   mushrooms, trimmed and sliced
3 eggs, at room temperature
salt and freshly ground black pepper

1 Melt the butter in a small omelette pan, add the mushrooms and cook until the juices run. Season with salt and pepper, remove from pan and set aside. Wipe the pan.

2 Break the eggs into a bowl, season and beat with a fork. Heat the pan over high heat, add a knob of butter and let it begin to brown. Pour in the beaten egg and stir briskly with the back of a fork.

3 When the eggs are two-thirds set, add the mushrooms and let the omelette finish cooking for 10–15 seconds.

4 Tap the handle of the omelette pan sharply with your fist to loosen the omelette from the pan, then fold and turn on to a plate. Serve with warm crusty bread and a simple green salad.

SUPPERS

Vegetable Pilau

A popular vegetable rice dish that
makes a tasty light supper.

INGREDIENTS

Serves 4–6

225 g/8 oz/1 cup basmati rice

30 ml/2 tbsp oil

2.5 ml/½ tsp cumin seeds

2 bay leaves

4 green cardamom pods

4 cloves

1 onion, finely chopped

1 carrot, finely diced

50 g/2 oz/⅓ cup frozen peas, thawed

50 g/2 oz/⅓ cup frozen sweetcorn, thawed

25 g/1 oz/¼ cup cashew nuts, lightly fried

1.5 ml/¼ tsp ground cumin

salt

1 Wash the basmati rice in several changes of cold water. Put into a bowl and cover with water. Leave to soak for about 30 minutes.

2 Heat the oil in a large frying pan and fry the cumin seeds for 2 minutes. Add the bay leaves, cardamoms and cloves and fry for a further 2 minutes.

3 Add the onion and fry for 5 minutes, until softened and lightly browned.

4 Stir in the carrot and cook for 3–4 minutes.

5 Drain the rice and add to the pan together with the peas, sweetcorn and cashew nuts. Fry for 4–5 minutes.

6 Add 475 ml/16 fl oz/2 cups water, ground cumin and salt. Bring to the boil, cover and simmer for 15 minutes over a low heat until all the water is absorbed. Leave to stand, covered, for 10 minutes, before serving.

Red Pepper Risotto

The character of this delicious risotto depends on the type of rice you use. With arborio rice, the risotto should be moist and creamy. If you use brown rice, reduce the amount of liquid for a drier dish with a nutty flavour.

INGREDIENTS

Serves 6

3 large red peppers
30 ml/2 tbsp olive oil
3 large garlic cloves, thinly sliced
1½ x 400 g/14 oz cans chopped tomatoes
2 bay leaves
1.2–1.5 litres/2–2½ pints/5–6¼ cups
    vegetable stock
450 g/1 lb/2½ cups arborio rice or
    brown rice
6 fresh basil leaves, snipped
salt and freshly ground black pepper

1 Preheat the grill. Put the peppers in a grill pan and grill until the skins are blackened and blistered all over. Put the peppers in a bowl, cover with several layers of damp kitchen paper and leave for 10 minutes. Peel off the skins, then slice the peppers, discarding the cores and seeds.

2 Heat the oil in a wide, shallow pan. Add the garlic and tomatoes and cook over a gentle heat for 5 minutes, then add the pepper slices and bay leaves. Stir well and cook for 15 minutes more, still over a gentle heat.

3 Pour the stock into a large, heavy-based saucepan and heat it to simmering point. Stir the rice into the vegetable mixture and cook for about 2 minutes, then add two or three ladlefuls of the hot stock. Cook, stirring occasionally, until all the stock has been absorbed into the rice.

4 Continue to add stock in this way, making sure each addition has been absorbed before pouring in the next. When the rice is tender, season with salt and pepper. Remove the pan from the heat, cover and leave to stand for 10 minutes before stirring in the basil and serving.

Risotto with Mushrooms

The addition of wild mushrooms gives this risotto a wonderfully authentic woody flavour.

INGREDIENTS

Serves 3–4

25 g/1 oz/⅓ cup dried wild mushrooms, preferably porcini

175 g/6 oz fresh cultivated mushrooms

juice of ½ lemon

75 g/3 oz/6 tbsp butter

30 ml/2 tbsp finely chopped parsley

900 ml/1½ pints/3¾ cups vegetable stock

30 ml/2 tbsp olive oil

1 small onion, finely chopped

275 g/10 oz/1½ cups medium grain risotto rice, such as arborio

120 ml/4 fl oz/½ cup dry white wine

45 ml/3 tbsp freshly grated Parmesan cheese

salt and freshly ground black pepper

sprig of flat leaf parsley, to garnish

1 Place the dried mushrooms in a small bowl with about 350 ml/12 fl oz/1½ cups warm water. Soak for at least 40 minutes. Rinse the mushrooms thoroughly. Filter the soaking water through a sieve lined with kitchen paper, and reserve.

2 Wipe the fresh mushrooms with a damp cloth and slice finely. Place in a bowl and toss with the lemon juice.

3 In a large heavy-based frying pan or casserole melt a third of the butter. Stir in the fresh sliced mushrooms and cook over moderate heat until they give up their juices and begin to brown. Stir in the parsley, cook for 30 seconds more, and remove to a side dish.

4 Place the stock in a saucepan. Add the mushroom water and simmer until needed.

5 Heat another third of the butter with the olive oil in the same pan the mushrooms were cooked in. Stir in the onion and cook until it is soft and golden. Add the rice, stirring for 1–2 minutes to coat it with the oils in the pan. Add the soaked and sautéed mushrooms and mix well.

6 Pour in the wine, raise the heat slightly, and cook over moderate heat until it evaporates.

7 Add one small ladleful of the hot broth. Over moderate heat cook until the broth is absorbed or evaporates, stirring the rice with a wooden spoon to prevent it sticking to the pan. Add a little more broth, and stir until the rice dries out again. Continue stirring and adding the liquid a little at a time. After abut 20 minutes taste the rice. Add salt and pepper.

8 Continue cooking, stirring and adding the liquid until the rice is *al dente*, or tender but still firm to the bite. The total cooking time of the risotto may be from 20–35 minutes. If you run out of broth, use hot water.

9 Remove the risotto pan from the heat. Stir in the remaining butter and the Parmesan. Grind in a little black pepper and taste again for salt. Allow the risotto to rest for 3–4 minutes before serving, garnished with a sprig of flat leaf parsley.

Parsnip, Aubergine and Cashew Biryani

Full of the flavours of India, this hearty supper dish is great for chilly winter evenings.

INGREDIENTS

Serves 4–6

1 small aubergine, sliced
275 g/10 oz basmati rice
3 parsnips
3 onions
2 garlic cloves
2.5 cm/1 in piece of fresh root ginger, peeled
about 60 ml/4 tbsp vegetable oil
175 g/6 oz unsalted cashew nuts
40 g/1½ oz sultanas
1 red pepper, seeded and sliced
5ml/1 tsp ground cumin
5 ml/1 tsp ground coriander
2.5 ml/½ tsp chilli powder
120 ml/4 fl oz/½ cup natural yogurt
300 ml/½ pint/1¼ cups vegetable stock
25 g/1 oz/2 tbsp butter
salt and freshly ground black pepper
2 hard-boiled eggs, quartered, and sprigs of fresh coriander, to garnish

1 Sprinkle the aubergine with salt and leave for 30 minutes. Rinse, pat dry and cut into bite-size pieces.

2 Soak the rice in a bowl of cold water for 40 minutes. Peel and core the parsnips. Cut into 1 cm/ ½ in pieces. Process 1 onion, the garlic and ginger in a food processor. Add 30–45 ml/2–3 tbsp water and process to a paste.

3 Finely slice the remaining onions. Heat 45 ml/3 tbsp of the oil in a large flameproof casserole and fry the onions gently for 10–15 minutes until they are soft and deep golden brown. Remove and drain.

4 Add 40 g/1½ oz of the cashew nuts to the pan and stir-fry for 2 minutes, checking that they do not burn. Add the sultanas and fry until they swell. Remove and drain on kitchen paper.

5 Add the aubergine and pepper to the pan and stir-fry for 4–5 minutes. Drain on kitchen paper. Fry the parsnips for 4–5 minutes. Stir in the remaining cashew nuts and fry for 1 minute. Transfer to the plate with the aubergine and set aside.

6 Add the remaining 15 ml/ 1 tbsp of oil to the pan. Add the onion paste. Cook, stirring, over a moderate heat for 4–5 minutes, until the mixture turns golden. Stir in the cumin, coriander and chilli powder. Cook, stirring, for 1 minute, then reduce the heat and add the yogurt.

7 Bring the mixture slowly to the boil and stir in the stock, parsnips, aubergine and peppers. Season with salt and pepper, cover and simmer for 30–40 minutes, until the parsnips are tender and then transfer to an ovenproof casserole.

8 Preheat the oven to 150°C/300°F/Gas 2. Drain the rice and add to 300 ml/½ pint/ 1¼ cups salted boiling water. Cook gently for 5–6 minutes, until the rice is tender but slightly under-cooked.

9 Drain the rice and pile it in a mound on top of the parsnips. Make a hole from the top to the base using the handle of a wooden spoon. Scatter the reserved fried onions, cashew nuts and sultanas over the rice and dot with butter. Cover with a double layer of foil and then secure in place with a lid.

10 Cook in the oven for 35–40 minutes. To serve, spoon the mixture on to a warmed serving dish and garnish with quartered eggs and sprigs of fresh coriander.

Leek, Mushroom and Lemon Risotto

A delicious risotto, packed full of flavour, this is a great recipe for an informal supper with friends.

INGREDIENTS

Serves 4

225 g/8 oz trimmed leeks
225 g/8 oz brown-cap mushrooms
30 ml/2 tbsp olive oil
3 garlic cloves, crushed
75 g/3 oz/6 tbsp butter
1 large onion, roughly chopped
350 g/12 oz/scant 1¾ cups arborio rice
1.2 litres/2 pints/5 cups hot
    vegetable stock
grated rind and juice of 1 lemon
50 g/2 oz/⅔ cup freshly grated
    Parmesan cheese
60 ml/4 tbsp mixed chopped fresh chives
    and flat leaf parsley
salt and freshly ground black pepper
lemon wedges and sprigs of flat leaf
    parsley, to serve

1 Wash the leeks well. Slice in half lengthways and roughly chop. Wipe the mushrooms with kitchen paper and roughly chop.

VARIATION

For a more zesty taste, you could substitute a lime for the lemon in this recipe.

2 Heat the oil in a large saucepan and cook the garlic for 1 minute. Add the leeks, mushrooms and plenty of seasoning and cook over a medium heat for about 10 minutes, or until softened and browned. Remove from the pan and set aside.

3 Add 25 g/1 oz/2 tbsp of the butter to the pan and cook the onion over medium heat for about 5 minutes.

4 Stir in the rice and cook for 1 minute. Add a ladleful of stock to the pan and cook gently, stirring occasionally, until all the liquid is absorbed.

5 Stir in more liquid as each ladleful is absorbed; this should take 20–25 minutes. The risotto will turn thick and creamy and the rice should be tender but not sticky.

6 Just before serving, stir in the leeks, mushrooms, remaining butter, grated lemon rind and 45 ml/3 tbsp of the juice, half the Parmesan and herbs. Adjust the seasoning and serve, sprinkled with the remaining Parmesan and herbs. Serve with lemon wedges and sprigs of flat leaf parsley.

Risotto alla Milanese

This traditional Italian risotto is rich and creamy, and deliciously flavoured with garlic, shavings of Parmesan and fresh parsley.

Serves 4

2 garlic cloves, crushed
60 ml/4 tbsp chopped fresh parsley
finely grated rind of 1 lemon

For the risotto

5 ml/1 tsp (or 1 sachet) saffron strands
25 g/1 oz/2 tbsp butter
1 large onion, finely chopped
275 g/10 oz/1½ cups arborio rice
150 ml/¼ pint/⅔ cup dry white wine
1 litre/1¾ pints/4 cups vegetable stock
Parmesan cheese shavings, to serve
salt and freshly ground black pepper

1 Mix together the garlic, parsley and lemon rind in a bowl. Reserve and set aside.

2 To make the risotto, put the saffron in a small bowl with 15 ml/1 tbsp boiling water and leave to stand while the saffron is infused. Melt the butter in a heavy-based frying saucepan and gently fry the onion for 5 minutes, until softened and golden.

3 Stir in the rice and cook for about 2 minutes until it becomes translucent. Add the wine and saffron mixture and cook for several minutes until all the wine is absorbed.

4 Add 600 ml/1 pint/2½ cups of the stock to the pan and simmer gently until the stock is absorbed, stirring frequently.

5 Gradually add more stock, a ladleful at a time, until the rice is tender. (The rice might be tender and creamy before you've added all the stock, so add it slowly towards the end of the cooking time.)

6 Season the risotto with salt and pepper and transfer to a serving dish. Scatter lavishly with shavings of Parmesan cheese and the garlic and parsley mixture.

Vegetable Chilli

This alternative to traditional chilli con carne is delicious served with brown rice.

INGREDIENTS

Serves 4

2 onions, chopped

1 garlic clove, crushed

3 sticks celery, chopped

1 green pepper, seeded and diced

225 g/8 oz mushrooms, sliced

2 courgettes, sliced

400 g/14 oz can red kidney beans, rinsed
   and drained

400 g/14 oz can chopped tomatoes

150 ml/¼ pint/⅔ cup passata

30 ml/2 tbsp tomato purée

15 ml/1 tbsp tomato ketchup

1 tsp each hot chilli powder, ground
   cumin and ground coriander

salt and freshly ground black pepper

natural yogurt and cayenne pepper,
   to serve

sprigs of fresh coriander, to garnish

1 Put the onions, garlic, celery, green pepper, mushrooms and courgettes in a large saucepan and mix together.

2 Add the kidney beans, tomatoes, passata, tomato purée and tomato ketchup.

3 Add the spices, season with salt and pepper and mix well.

4 Cover, bring to the boil and simmer for 20–30 minutes, stirring occasionally, until the vegetables are tender. Serve with natural yogurt, sprinkled with cayenne pepper. Garnish with fresh coriander sprigs.

Wholemeal Pasta with Caraway Cabbage

Crunchy cabbage and Brussels sprouts are the perfect partners for pasta in this healthy dish.

INGREDIENTS

Serves 6

90 ml/6 tbsp olive oil or sunflower oil

3 onions, roughly chopped

350 g/12 oz round white cabbage, roughly chopped

350 g/12 oz Brussels sprouts, trimmed and halved

10 ml/2 tsp caraway seeds

15 ml/1 tbsp chopped fresh dill

400 ml/14 fl oz/1⅔ cups vegetable stock

200 g/7 oz/1¼ cups fresh or dried whole-wheat pasta spirals

salt and freshly ground black pepper

fresh dill sprigs, to garnish

1 Heat the oil in a large saucepan and fry the onions over a low heat for 10 minutes, until softened.

2 Add the cabbage and Brussels sprouts and cook for 2–3 minutes, then stir in the caraway seeds and dill. Pour in the stock and season with salt and pepper. Cover and simmer for 5–10 minutes, until the cabbage and sprouts are crisp-tender.

3 Meanwhile, cook the pasta in a pan of lightly salted boiling water, following the package instructions, until just tender.

4 Drain the pasta, tip it into a bowl and add the cabbage mixture. Toss lightly, adjust the seasoning, garnish with dill and serve immediately.

Cauliflower and Broccoli with Tomato Sauce

A tasty alternative to that old favourite, cauliflower cheese. The addition of broccoli to the cauliflower gives extra colour and texture to this old favourite.

INGREDIENTS

Serves 6

1 onion, finely chopped

400 g/14 oz can chopped tomatoes

45 ml/3 tbsp tomato purée

20 g/¾ oz/3 tbsp wholemeal flour

300 ml/½ pint/1¼ cups skimmed milk

300 ml/½ pint/1¼ cups water

1 kg/2¼ lb/6 cups mixed cauliflower and broccoli florets

salt and freshly ground black pepper

1 Mix the onion, tomatoes and tomato purée in a small saucepan. Bring to the boil, lower the heat and simmer gently for 15–20 minutes.

2 Mix the flour to a paste with a little of the milk. Stir the paste into the tomato mixture, then gradually add the remaining milk and water.

3 Stir the mixture constantly, until it boils and thickens. Season with salt and pepper. Keep the sauce hot.

4 Steam the cauliflower and broccoli over boiling water for 5–7 minutes or until the florets are just tender. Tip into a dish, pour over the tomato sauce and serve with extra pepper sprinkled over the top, if liked.

Mushroom Bolognese

*A quick — and exceedingly tasty —
vegetarian version of the classic
Italian dish. This dish is easy to
prepare and makes a very
satisfying meal.*

INGREDIENTS

Serves 4

450 g/1 lb mushrooms
15 ml/1 tbsp olive oil
1 onion, chopped
1 garlic clove, crushed
15 ml/1 tbsp tomato purée
400 g/14 oz can chopped tomatoes
45 ml/3 tbsp chopped fresh oregano
450 g/1 lb fresh pasta
salt and freshly ground black pepper
Parmesan cheese, to serve

1 Trim the mushroom stems
neatly. Then cut each
mushroom into quarters.

2 Heat the oil in a large pan. Add
the chopped onion and garlic
and cook for 2–3 minutes.

3 Add the mushrooms to the
pan and cook over a high heat
for about 3–4 minutes, stirring
occasionally.

4 Stir in the tomato purée,
chopped tomatoes and 15 ml/
1 tbsp of the oregano. Lower the
heat, cover and then cook for
about 5 minutes.

5 Meanwhile, bring a large pan
of salted water to the boil.
Cook the pasta for 2–3 minutes,
until just tender.

6 Season the bolognese sauce
with salt and pepper. Drain
the pasta, turn it into a bowl and
add the mushroom mixture. Toss
to mix well. Serve in individual
bowls, topped with shavings of
fresh Parmesan and the remaining
chopped fresh oregano.

COOK'S TIP

If you prefer to use dried pasta,
make this the first thing that you
cook. It will take 10–12 minutes,
during which time you can make
the mushroom mixture. Use
350 g/12 oz dried pasta.

Broccoli and Ricotta Cannelloni

A fabulous pasta dish that looks very impressive but is actually quite quick and simple to prepare, and tastes wonderful.

Serves 4

10 ml/2 tsp olive oil

12 dried cannelloni tubes, 7.5 cm/3 in long

450 g/1 lb/4 cups broccoli florets

75 g/3 oz/1½ cups fresh breadcrumbs

150 ml/¼ pint/⅔ cup milk

60 ml/4 tbsp olive oil, plus extra for brushing

225 g/8 oz/1 cup ricotta cheese

pinch of grated nutmeg

90 ml/6 tbsp grated Parmesan or Pecorino cheese

30 ml/2 tbsp pine nuts

salt and freshly ground black pepper

For the tomato sauce

30 ml/2 tbsp olive oil

1 onion, finely chopped

1 garlic clove, crushed

2 x 400 g/14 oz cans chopped tomatoes

15 ml/1 tbsp tomato purée

4 black olives, stoned and chopped

5 ml/1 tsp dried thyme

1 Preheat the oven to 190°C/375°F/Gas 5. Lightly grease four ovenproof dishes with olive oil.

2 Bring a large saucepan of water to the boil, add the olive oil to the water to prevent the pasta from sticking together and simmer the cannelloni, uncovered, for 6–7 minutes, or until it is nearly cooked.

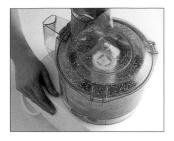

3 Meanwhile, steam or boil the broccoli for 10 minutes, until tender. Drain the pasta, rinse under cold water and reserve. Drain the broccoli and leave to cool, then place in a food processor or blender and process until smooth. Set aside.

4 Place the breadcrumbs in a bowl, add the milk and oil and stir until softened. Add the ricotta, broccoli purée, nutmeg and 60 ml/4 tbsp of the Parmesan or Pecorino cheese. Season with salt and pepper then set aside.

5 To make the sauce, heat the oil in a frying pan and add the onions and garlic. Fry for 5–6 minutes, until softened, then stir in the tomatoes, tomato purée, black olives and thyme. Season with salt and pepper. Boil rapidly for 2–3 minutes then pour into the four ovenproof dishes.

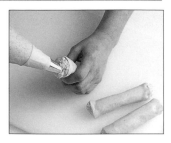

6 Spoon the cheese mixture into a piping bag fitted with a 1 cm/½ in nozzle. Carefully open the cannelloni tubes. Standing each one upright on a board, pipe the filling into each tube. Divide the tubes equally between the four dishes and lay them in rows in the tomato sauce.

7 Brush the tops of the cannelloni with a little olive oil and sprinkle over the remaining Parmesan or Pecorino cheese and pine nuts. Bake in the oven for about 25–30 minutes, until golden.

COOK'S TIP

If you don't have cannelloni tubes, you can cook lasagne sheets until *al dente*, spoon the mixture along one short edge of the sheet and roll it up to encase the filling.

Spiced Tofu Stir-fry

The colours in this aromatic stir-fry are as pleasing to the eye as the flavours are to the palate. Serve with noodles or egg-fried rice.

Serves 4

10 ml/2 tsp ground cumin

15 ml/1 tbsp paprika

5 ml/1 tsp ground ginger

good pinch of cayenne pepper

15 ml/1 tbsp caster sugar

275 g/10 oz tofu (beancurd)

60 ml/4 tbsp oil

2 garlic cloves, crushed

1 bunch spring onions, sliced

1 red pepper, seeded and sliced

1 yellow pepper, seeded and sliced

225g/8 oz/generous 3 cups brown-cap
    mushrooms, halved or quartered
    if necessary

1 large courgette, sliced

115 g/4 oz fine green beans, halved

50 g/2 oz/scant ½ cup pine nuts

15 ml/1 tbsp lime juice

15ml/1 tbsp clear honey

salt and pepper

1 Mix together the cumin, paprika, ginger, cayenne and sugar with plenty of seasoning. Cut the tofu into cubes and coat them in the spice mixture.

2 Heat some of the oil in a wok or large frying pan. Cook the tofu over a high heat for 3–4 minutes, turning occasionally (take care not to break up the tofu too much). Remove with a slotted spoon. Wipe out the pan with kitchen paper.

3 Add the remaining oil to the pan and cook the garlic and spring onions for 3 minutes. Add the remaining vegetables and cook over a medium heat for 6 minutes, or until beginning to soften and turn golden. Season well.

4 Return the tofu to the pan with the pine nuts, lime juice and honey. Heat through and serve immediately.

Butternut Squash and Sage Pizza

The combination of sweet butternut squash, sage and sharp goat's cheese works wonderfully on this pizza.

INGREDIENTS

Serves 4

2.5 ml/½ tsp active dried yeast

pinch of granulated sugar

450 g/1 lb/4 cups strong white flour

5 ml/1 tsp salt

30 ml/2 tbsp olive oil

15 g/½ oz/1 tbsp butter

30 ml/2 tbsp olive oil

2 shallots, finely chopped

1 butternut squash, peeled, seeded and
    cubed, about 450 g/1 lb prepared weight

16 sage leaves

2 x 400 g/14 oz cans fresh tomato sauce

115 g/4 oz/1 cup mozzarella cheese, sliced

115 g/4 oz/½ cup firm goat's cheese

salt and freshly ground black pepper

1 Put 300 ml/½ pint/1¼ cups warm water in a measuring jug. Add the yeast and sugar and leave for 5–10 minutes, until it is frothy.

2 Sift the flour and salt into a large bowl and make a well in the centre. Gradually pour in the yeast mixture and the olive oil. Mix to make a smooth dough. Knead on a lightly floured surface for about 10 minutes until smooth, springy and elastic. Place the dough in a floured bowl, cover and leave to rise in a warm place for 1½ hours.

3 Preheat the oven to 200°C/400°F/Gas 6. Oil four baking sheets. Put the butter and oil in a roasting tin and heat in the oven for a few minutes. Add the shallots, squash and half the sage leaves. Toss to coat. Roast for 15–20 minutes, until tender.

4 Raise the oven temperature to 220°C/425°F/Gas 7. Divide the dough into four equal pieces and roll out each piece on a floured surface to a 25 cm/10 in round.

5 Transfer each round to a baking sheet and spread with tomato sauce, leaving a 1 cm/½ in border all around. Spoon the squash and shallot mixture over the top.

6 Arrange the mozzarella over the squash mixture and crumble the goat's cheese over. Scatter the remaining sage leaves over and season with plenty of salt and pepper. Bake for 15–20 minutes, until the cheese has melted and the crusts are golden.

Aubergine, Shallot and Tomato Calzone

Aubergines, shallots and sun-dried tomatoes make an unusual filling for calzone. Add more or less red chilli flakes, depending on how fiery you like your food.

Serves 2

1.5 ml/¼ tsp active dried yeast
pinch of granulated sugar
225 g/8 oz/2 cups strong white flour
1 tsp salt
60 ml/4 tbsp olive oil
4 baby aubergines
3 shallots, chopped
1 garlic clove, chopped
50 g/2 oz (drained weight) sun-dried
   tomatoes in oil, chopped
1.5 ml/¼ tsp dried red chilli flakes
10 ml/2 tsp chopped fresh thyme
75 g/3 oz mozzarella cheese, cubed
salt and freshly ground black pepper
15–30 ml/1–2 tbsp freshly grated
   Parmesan cheese, to serve

1 To make the dough, put 150 ml/¼ pint/⅔ cup warm water in a measuring jug. Add the yeast and sugar and leave for 5–10 minutes, until frothy.

2 Sift the flour and salt into a large bowl and make a well in the centre. Gradually pour in the yeast mixture and 15 ml/1 tbsp oil. Mix to make a smooth dough. Knead the dough on a lightly floured surface for 10 minutes until smooth. The dough should be springy and elastic.

3 Place the dough in a floured bowl, cover and leave to rise in a warm place for 1½ hours. Preheat the oven to 220°C/425°F/ Gas 7. Trim the aubergines, then cut into small cubes.

4 Heat 15 ml/1 tbsp of the oil in a frying pan and cook the shallots until soft. Add the aubergines, garlic, sun-dried tomatoes, red chilli flakes, thyme and seasoning. Cook for about 4–5 minutes, stirring frequently, until the aubergine is beginning to soften.

5 Divide the pizza dough in half and roll out each piece on a lightly floured surface to an 18 cm/7 in circle.

6 Spread the aubergine mixture over half of each round, leaving a 2.5 cm/1 in border, then scatter over the mozzarella.

7 Dampen the edges with water, then fold over the other half of dough to enclose the filling. Press the edges firmly together to seal. Place the calzones on two greased baking sheets.

8 Brush with half the remaining olive oil and make a small hole in the top of each to allow the steam to escape. Bake for about 15–20 minutes until golden. Remove from the oven and brush with the remaining oil. Sprinkle over the Parmesan cheese and serve immediately.

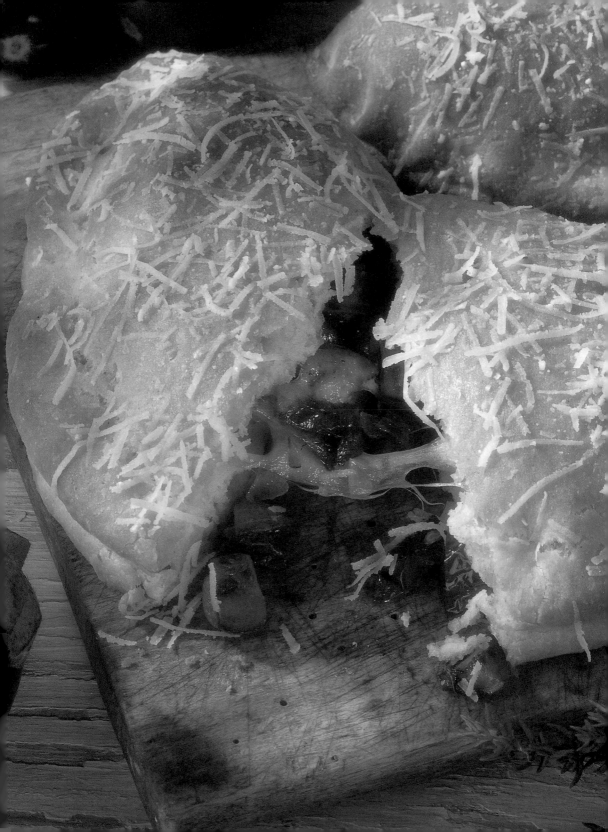

Ravioli with Ricotta and Spinach

Home-made ravioli are fun to make, and can be stuffed with different cheese or vegetable fillings. This filling is particularly easy to make.

INGREDIENTS

Serves 4

400 g/14 oz fresh spinach or 175 g/6 oz frozen spinach

175 g/6 oz/³⁄₄ cup ricotta cheese

1 egg

50 g/2 oz/½ cup grated Parmesan cheese

pinch of grated nutmeg

egg pasta sheets

salt and freshly ground black pepper

For the pasta

210 g/7½ oz/1½ cups flour

3 eggs

For the sauce

75 g/3 oz/6 tbsp butter

5–6 sprigs of fresh sage

1 Wash the fresh spinach well in several changes of water. Place in a saucepan, cover and cook until tender, about 5 minutes. Drain. Cook frozen spinach according to the package instructions. When cool, squeeze out as much moisture as possible. Chop finely.

2 Combine the chopped spinach with the ricotta, egg, Parmesan and nutmeg. Season with salt and pepper. Cover and set aside.

3 To make the pasta, place the flour in the centre of a clean smooth work surface. Make a well in the middle. Break the eggs into the well. Add a pinch of salt.

4 Start beating the eggs with a fork, gradually drawing the flour from the inside walls of the well. As the paste thickens, continue mixing with your hands.

5 Incorporate as much flour as possible until the mixture forms a mass. It will still be lumpy. If it still sticks to your hands, add a little more flour. Set the dough aside. Scrape off the dough from the work surface until it is smooth.

6 Lightly flour the work surface. Knead the dough. Work for about 10 minutes, or until the dough is smooth and elastic.

7 Divide the dough in half. Flour the rolling pin and the work surface. Pat the dough into a disc and begin rolling out into a flat circle. Roll until it is about 3mm ⅛ in thick. Do the same for the second half of the dough.

8 Cut the dough into sheets. Place small teaspoons of filling along the pasta in rows 5 cm/ 2 in apart. Cover with another sheet of pasta, pressing down gently to expel any air pockets.

9 Use a fluted pastry wheel to cut between the rows to form small squares with filling in the centre of each. If the edges do not stick well, moisten with milk or water and press together.

10 Place the ravioli on a lightly floured surface and allow to dry for at least 30 minutes. Turn occasionally so they are completely dry on both sides. Bring a large pan of salted water to the boil.

11 Heat the butter and sage together over very low heat, taking care that the butter melts but does not darken.

12 Drop the ravioli into the boiling water. Stir gently to prevent them from sticking together. They will be cooked in very little time, about 4–5 minutes. Drain carefully and arrange in individual serving dishes. Spoon on the sauce and serve at once.

Coriander Ravioli with Pumpkin Filling

A stunning pasta that combines fresh herbs with a superb creamy pumpkin and roast garlic filling.

INGREDIENTS

Serves 4–6

200 g/7 oz/scant 1 cup strong unbleached
   white flour
2 eggs
pinch of salt
45 ml/3 tbsp chopped fresh coriander
sprigs of fresh coriander, to garnish

For the filling
4 garlic cloves in their skins
450 g/1 lb pumpkin, peeled and
   seeds removed
115 g/4 oz/½ cup ricotta cheese
4 halves sun-dried tomatoes in olive oil,
   drained and finely chopped (reserve
   30 ml/2 tbsp of the oil)
freshly ground black pepper

1 Place the flour, eggs, salt and coriander into a food processor. Pulse until combined.

2 Knead the dough on a lightly floured board until smooth.

3 Wrap the dough in clear film and leave to rest in the fridge for 20–30 minutes.

4 Preheat the oven to 200°C/400°F/Gas 6. Place the garlic cloves on a baking sheet and bake for 10 minutes, until softened. Steam the pumpkin for 5–8 minutes, until tender, and drain well.

5 Peel the garlic cloves and mash into the pumpkin together with the ricotta and drained sun-dried tomatoes. Season with plenty of black pepper.

6 Divide the pasta into 4 pieces and flatten slightly. Using a pasta machine, on its thinnest setting, roll out each piece. Leave the sheets of pasta on a clean dish towel until slightly dried.

7 Using a 7.5 cm/3 in crinkle-edged round cutter, stamp out 36 rounds.

8 Top 18 of the rounds with a teaspoonful of the pumpkin mixture, brush the edges with water and place another round of pasta on top. Press firmly around the edges to seal. Bring a large pan of water to the boil, add the ravioli and cook for 3–4 minutes. Drain well and toss into the reserved tomato oil. Add pepper and serve garnished with coriander sprigs.

VARIATION

For an alternative filling you could substitute the ricotta cheese with 25 g/1 oz grated Parmesan cheese mixed with 115 g/4 oz cottage cheese. Serve with shavings of Parmesan.

Purée of Lentils with Baked Eggs

This unusual dish makes an
excellent supper. For a nutty flavour
you could add a 400 g/14 oz can of
unsweetened chestnut purée to the
lentil mixture.

INGREDIENTS

Serves 4

450 g/1 lb/2 cups washed brown lentils

3 leeks, thinly sliced

10 ml/2 tsp coriander seeds, crushed

15 ml/1 tbsp chopped fresh coriander

30 ml/2 tbsp chopped fresh mint

15 ml/1 tbsp red wine vinegar

1 litre/1¾ pints/4 cups vegetable stock

4 eggs

salt and freshly ground black pepper

generous handful of fresh parsley,
   chopped, to garnish

1 Put the lentils in a deep
saucepan. Add the leeks,
coriander seeds, fresh coriander,
mint, vinegar and stock. Bring to
the boil, then lower the heat and
simmer for 30–40 minutes, until
the lentils are cooked and have
absorbed all the liquid.

2 Preheat the oven to
180°C/350°F/Gas 4.

3 Season the lentils with salt
and pepper and mix well.
Spread out in four lightly greased
baking dishes.

4 Using the back of a spoon,
make a hollow in the lentil
mixture in each dish. Break an egg
into each hollow. Cover the dishes
with foil and bake for 15–20
minutes, or until the egg whites are
set and the yolks are still soft.
Sprinkle with plenty of parsley and
serve at once.

Harvest Vegetable and Lentil Casserole

Take advantage of root vegetables in season to produce a hearty dish that's not only full of natural goodness but delicious too.

INGREDIENTS

Serves 6

15 ml/1 tbsp sunflower oil
2 leeks, sliced
1 garlic clove, crushed
4 celery sticks, chopped
2 carrots, sliced
2 parsnips, diced
1 sweet potato, diced
225 g/8 oz swede, diced
175 g/6 oz whole brown or green lentils
450 g/1 lb tomatoes, skinned, seeded
   and chopped
15 ml/1 tbsp chopped fresh thyme
15 ml/1 tbsp chopped fresh marjoram
900 ml/1½ pints/3¾ cups vegetable stock
15 ml/1 tbsp cornflour
salt and freshly ground black pepper
sprigs of fresh thyme, to garnish

1 Preheat the oven to 180°C/350°F/Gas 4. Heat the oil in a flameproof casserole over moderate heat. Add the leeks, garlic and celery and cook gently for 3 minutes.

2 Add the carrots, parsnips, sweet potato, swede, lentils, tomatoes, herbs, stock and seasoning. Stir well. Bring to the boil, stirring occasionally.

3 Cover and bake in the oven for about 50 minutes, until the vegetables and the lentils are cooked and tender. While it is cooking, remove the casserole from the oven and stir the vegetable mixture once or twice so that it is evenly cooked.

4 Remove the casserole from the oven. Blend the cornflour with 45 ml/3 tbsp water in a bowl. Stir into the casserole and heat, stirring continuously, until the mixture comes to the boil and thickens. Simmer gently for 2 minutes.

5 Spoon the vegetable mixture into bowls and serve garnished with thyme sprigs.

Baked Vegetable Lasagne

This recipe uses fresh vegetables and herbs to create a delicious version of the classic favourite.

INGREDIENTS

Serves 8

15–18 fresh or dried lasagne sheets

30 ml/2 tbsp olive oil

1 medium onion, very finely chopped

500 g/1¼ lb tomatoes, fresh or
    canned, chopped

675 g/1½ lb cultivated or wild
    mushrooms, or a combination of both

75 g/3 oz/6 tbsp butter

2 garlic cloves, finely chopped

juice of ½ lemon

1 litre/1¾ pints/4 cups ready-made
    béchamel sauce

175 g/6 oz/1½ cups freshly grated
    Parmesan or Cheddar cheese, or a
    combination of both

salt and freshly ground black pepper

1 Butter a large, shallow, ovenproof baking dish, preferably rectangular or square.

2 Heat the oil in a small frying pan and sauté the onion until translucent. Add the chopped tomatoes and cook for 6–8 minutes, stirring often. Season with salt and pepper and set aside.

3 Wipe the mushrooms carefully with a damp cloth. Slice finely. Heat half the butter in a frying pan and, when it is bubbling, add the mushrooms. Cook until the mushrooms start to exude their juice. Add the garlic and lemon juice and season with salt and pepper.

4 Cook the mushroom mixture until the liquids have almost all evaporated and the mushrooms are starting to brown. Set aside.

5 Preheat the oven to 200°C/ 400°F/Gas 6. Bring a pan of water to the boil and place a bowl of cold water near the stove. Add salt to the rapidly boiling water.

6 Drop in 3 or 4 of the lasagne sheets. Cook for about 30 seconds. Remove them from the pan, and drop them into the cold water for 30 seconds. Remove and lay out to dry. Continue with the remaining pasta. If using pre-cooked lasagne, skip this step.

7 To assemble the lasagne, have all the elements at hand: the baking dish, fillings, pasta, cheeses and butter. Spread one large spoonful of the béchamel sauce over the bottom of the dish. Arrange a layer of pasta in the dish, cutting it with a sharp knife so that it fits well. Cover the pasta with a thin layer of mushrooms, then one of béchamel sauce. Sprinkle with a little cheese.

8 Make another layer of pasta, spread with a thin layer of tomatoes then one of béchamel. Sprinkle with cheese.

9 Repeat the layers in the same order, ending with a layer of pasta and béchamel. Do not make more than about 6 layers. Use the pasta trimmings to patch any gaps in the pasta. Sprinkle with cheese and dot with the remaining butter.

10 Bake for 20 minutes. Remove from the oven and allow to stand for 5 minutes.

COOK'S TIP

Fresh pasta is not necessarily better than dried but it takes much less time to cook as it still contains moisture. Fresh pasta should always be stored in the fridge or freezer until ready for cooking.

Chilli, Tomato and Spinach Pizza

This richly flavoured topping with a hint of spice makes a colourful and satisfying pizza.

INGREDIENTS

Serves 3

1–2 fresh red chillies
45 ml/3 tbsp tomato oil (from jar of
   sun-dried tomatoes)
1 onion, chopped
2 garlic cloves, chopped
50 g/2 oz (drained weight) sun-dried
   tomatoes in oil
400 g/14 oz can chopped tomatoes
15 ml/1 tbsp tomato purée
175 g/6 oz fresh spinach
1 pizza base, 25–30 cm/10–12 in
   in diameter
75 g/3 oz smoked Bavarian cheese, grated
75 g/3 oz mature Cheddar, grated
salt and freshly ground black pepper

1 Seed and finely chop the chillies.

2 Heat 30 ml/2 tbsp of the tomato oil in a saucepan, add the onion, garlic and chillies and fry gently for about 5 minutes, until they are soft.

3 Roughly chop the sun-dried tomatoes. Add to the pan with the chopped tomatoes and tomato purée. Season with salt and pepper. Simmer, uncovered, stirring occasionally, for 15 minutes.

4 Remove the stalks from the spinach and wash the leaves in plenty of cold water. Drain well and pat dry with kitchen paper. Roughly chop the spinach.

5 Stir the spinach into the sauce. Cook, stirring, for a further 5–10 minutes until the spinach has wilted and no excess moisture remains. Leave to cool.

6 Meanwhile, preheat the oven to 220°C/425°F/Gas 7. Brush the pizza base with the remaining tomato oil, then spoon over the sauce. Sprinkle over the grated cheeses and bake in the oven for 15–20 minutes, until crisp and golden. Serve immediately.

COOK'S TIP

The smoked cheese used in this pizza topping creates an unusual rich flavour, which complements the hot, spicy chillies. If you want to heighten this taste, substitute the Cheddar with another 75 g/3 oz of the smoked Bavarian cheese.

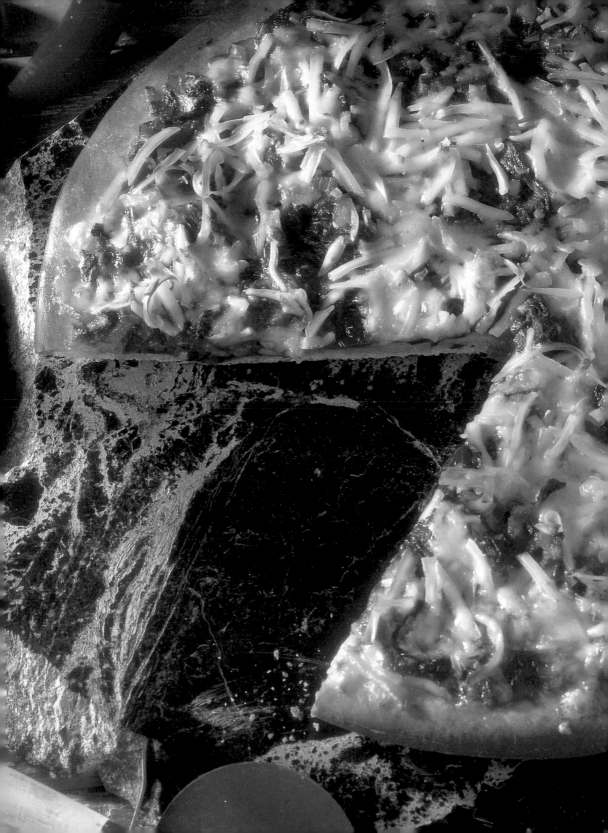

Tagliatelle with Spinach Gnocchi

Gnocchi are extremely smooth and light and make a delicious accompaniment to this pasta dish.

INGREDIENTS

Serves 4–6

450 g/1 lb mixed flavoured tagliatelle
shavings of Parmesan cheese, to garnish

For the spinach gnocchi

450 g/1 lb frozen chopped spinach
1 small onion, finely chopped
1 garlic clove, crushed
1.5 ml/¼ tsp ground nutmeg
400 g/14 oz low-fat cottage cheese
115 g/4 oz dried white breadcrumbs
75 g/3 oz semolina or plain flour
50 g/2 oz grated Parmesan cheese
3 egg whites

For the tomato sauce

1 onion, finely chopped
1 stick celery, finely chopped
1 red pepper, seeded and diced
1 garlic clove, crushed
150 ml/¼ pint/⅔ cup vegetable stock
400 g/14 oz can tomatoes
15 ml/1 tbsp tomato purée
10 ml/2 tsp caster sugar
5 ml/1 tsp dried oregano
salt and freshly ground black pepper

1 To make the tomato sauce, put the chopped onion, celery, pepper and garlic into a non-stick pan. Add the stock, bring to the boil and cook for 5 minutes or until tender.

2 Add the tomatoes, tomato purée, sugar and oregano. Season to taste, bring to the boil and simmer for 30 minutes until thick, stirring occasionally.

3 Put the spinach, onion and garlic into a saucepan, cover and cook until the spinach is defrosted. Remove the lid and increase the heat. Season with salt, pepper and nutmeg. Cool in a bowl. Mix in the remaining ingredients. Shape into about 24 ovals and refrigerate for 30 minutes.

4 Cook the gnocchi in boiling salted water for about 5 minutes. Remove with a slotted spoon and drain. Cook the tagliatelle in a pan of boiling salted water until *al dente*. Drain. Transfer to serving plates, top with gnocchi, the tomato sauce and shavings of Parmesan cheese.

Pizza with Fresh Vegetables

This pizza can be made with any combination of fresh vegetables. Most will benefit from being blanched or sautéed before being baked on the pizza.

INGREDIENTS

Serves 4

400 g/14 oz peeled plum tomatoes, fresh or canned, weighed whole, without extra juice

2 medium broccoli spears

225 g/8 oz fresh asparagus

2 small courgettes

75 ml/5 tbsp olive oil

50 g/2 oz/⅓ cup shelled peas, fresh or frozen

4 spring onions, sliced

1 pizza base, 25–30 cm/10–12 in in diameter

75 g/3 oz/⅓ cup mozzarella cheese, cut into small dice

10 leaves fresh basil, torn into pieces

2 cloves garlic, finely chopped

salt and freshly ground black pepper

1 Preheat the oven to 240°C/475°F/Gas 9 for at least 20 minutes before baking the pizza. Strain the tomatoes through the medium hole of a food mill, scraping in all the pulp.

2 Peel the broccoli stems and asparagus, and blanch with the courgettes in a pan of boiling water for 4–5 minutes. Drain. Cut into bite-size pieces and slice the courgettes lengthways.

3 Heat 30 ml/2 tbsp of the olive oil in a small saucepan. Stir in the peas and spring onions and cook for 5–6 minutes, stirring often. Remove from the heat.

4 Spread the puréed tomatoes on to the pizza dough, leaving the rim uncovered. Add the other vegetables, spreading them evenly over the tomatoes.

5 Sprinkle with the mozzarella, basil, garlic, salt and pepper and remaining olive oil. Immediately place the pizza in the oven. Bake for about 20 minutes, or until the crust is golden brown and the cheese has melted.

Ricotta and Fontina Pizza

The earthy flavours of the mixed mushrooms perfectly complement the two creamy cheeses in this delectable recipe.

INGREDIENTS

Serves 4

2.5 ml/½ tsp active dried yeast
pinch of granulated sugar
450 g/1 lb/4 cups strong white flour
5 ml/1 tsp salt
30 ml/2 tbsp olive oil

For the tomato sauce

400 g/14 oz can chopped tomatoes
150 ml/¼ pint/⅔ cup passata
1 large garlic clove, finely chopped
5 ml/1 tsp dried oregano
1 bay leaf
10 ml/2 tsp malt vinegar
salt and freshly ground black pepper

For the topping

30 ml/2 tbsp olive oil
1 garlic clove, finely chopped
350 g/12 oz mixed mushrooms (chestnut,
    flat or button), sliced
30 ml/2 tbsp chopped fresh oregano, plus
    whole leaves, to garnish
250 g/9 oz/generous 1 cup ricotta cheese
225 g/8 oz Fontina cheese, sliced

1 To make the dough, put 300 ml/½ pint/1¼ cups warm water in a measuring jug. Add the yeast and sugar and leave for 5–10 minutes, until frothy.

2 Sift the flour and salt into a large bowl and make a well in the centre. Gradually pour in the yeast mixture and the olive oil. Mix to make a smooth dough. Knead on a lightly floured surface for about 10 minutes until smooth, springy and elastic. Place the dough in a floured bowl, cover and leave to rise in a warm place for 1½ hours.

3 Meanwhile, make the tomato sauce. Put all the ingredients in a saucepan, cover and bring to the boil. Lower the heat, remove the lid and simmer for 20 minutes, stirring occasionally, until reduced.

4 To make the topping, heat the oil in a frying pan. Add the garlic and mushrooms and season with salt and pepper. Cook, stirring, for about 5 minutes, or until the mushrooms are tender and golden. Set aside.

5 Preheat the oven to 220°C/425°F/Gas 7. Brush four baking sheets with oil. Knead the dough for 2 minutes, then divide into four equal pieces. Roll out each piece to a 25 cm/10 in round and place on a baking sheet.

6 Spoon the tomato sauce over each dough round. Brush the edge with a little olive oil. Add the mushrooms, oregano and cheeses. Season to taste. Bake for about 15 minutes, until golden brown and crisp. Garnish with oregano leaves.

COOK'S TIP

To freeze, allow to cool to room temperature after baking. Wrap in foil and freeeze. Thaw completely and place in a warm oven before serving.

Red Cabbage and Apple Casserole

The brilliant colour and pungent flavour make this an excellent winter dish. Serve it with plenty of rye bread.

INGREDIENTS

Serves 6

3 onions, chopped

2 fennel bulbs, roughly chopped

675 g/1½ lb red cabbage

30 ml/2 tbsp caraway seeds

3 large, tart eating apples or 1 large
   cooking apple

300 ml/½ pint/1¼ cups natural yogurt

15 ml/1 tbsp creamed horseradish sauce

salt and freshly ground black pepper

crusty rye bread, to serve

1 Preheat the oven to 150°C/300°F/Gas 2. Shred the cabbage finely, discarding any tough stalks. Mix with the onions, fennel and caraway seeds in a large bowl. Peel, core and chop the apples then stir them into the cabbage mixture. Transfer the ingredients to a casserole dish.

2 Mix the yogurt with the creamed horseradish sauce. Stir the yogurt and horseradish mixture into the casserole, season with salt and pepper and cover tightly.

3 Bake for 1½ hours, stirring once or twice during cooking. Serve hot, with crusty bread.

Mixed Vegetables with Artichokes

Baking a vegetable medley in the oven is a wonderfully easy way of producing a quick and simple, wholesome mid-week meal.

INGREDIENTS

Serves 4

30 ml/2 tbsp olive oil

675 g/1½ lb frozen broad beans

4 turnips, peeled and sliced

4 leeks, sliced

1 red pepper, seeded and sliced

200 g/7 oz fresh spinach leaves or 115 g/
   4 oz frozen spinach

2 x 400 g/14 oz cans artichoke
   hearts, drained

60 ml/4 tbsp pumpkin seeds

soy sauce

salt and freshly ground black pepper

2 Cover the casserole and bake the vegetables for 30–40 minutes, or until the turnips are slightly soft.

1 Preheat the oven to 180°C/350°F/Gas 4. Pour the olive oil into a casserole. Cook the broad beans in a saucepan of boiling lightly salted water for about 10 minutes. Drain the broad beans and place them in the casserole with the turnips, leeks, red pepper, spinach and canned artichoke hearts.

3 Stir in the pumpkin seeds and soy sauce to taste. Season with salt and pepper to taste and serve immediately.

Vegetable Moussaka

*This is a really flavoursome main
course dish. It can be served with
warm fresh bread for a hearty,
satisfying meal.*

INGREDIENTS

Serves 6

450 g/1 lb aubergines, sliced

115 g/4 oz whole green lentils

600 ml/1 pint/2½ cups vegetable stock

1 bay leaf

45 ml/3 tbsp olive oil

1 onion, sliced

1 garlic clove, crushed

225 g/8 oz mushrooms, sliced

400 g/14 oz can chick-peas, rinsed
    and drained

400 g/14 oz can chopped tomatoes

30 ml/2 tbsp tomato purée

10 ml/2 tsp dried herbes de Provence

300 ml/½ pint/1¼ cups natural yogurt

3 eggs

50 g/2 oz/½ cup mature Cheddar
    cheese, grated

salt and freshly ground black pepper

sprigs of fresh flat leaf parsley, to garnish

1 Sprinkle the aubergine slices
with salt and place in a
colander. Cover and place a weight
on top. Leave for at least 30
minutes, to allow the bitter juices
to be extracted.

2 Meanwhile, place the lentils,
stock and bay leaf in a
saucepan, cover, bring to the boil
and simmer for about 20 minutes,
until the lentils are just tender but
not mushy. Drain thoroughly and
keep warm.

3 Heat 15 ml/1 tbsp of the oil in
a large saucepan, add the
onion and garlic and cook for
5 minutes, stirring. Stir in the
lentils, mushrooms, chick-peas,
tomatoes, tomato purée, herbs and
45 ml/3 tbsp water. Bring to the
boil, cover and simmer gently for
10 minutes, stirring occasionally.

4 Preheat the oven to
180°C/350°F/Gas 4. Rinse the
aubergine slices, drain and pat dry.
Heat the remaining oil in a frying
pan and fry the slices in batches for
3–4 minutes, turning once so both
sides are browned.

5 Season the lentil mixture with
salt and pepper. Arrange a
layer of aubergine slices in the
bottom of a large, shallow,
ovenproof dish or roasting tin,
then spoon over a layer of the
lentil mixture. Continue the layers
until all the aubergine slices and
lentil mixture are used up.

6 Beat the yogurt, eggs, salt and
pepper together and pour the
mixture over the dish. Sprinkle
generously with the grated
Cheddar cheese and bake for about
45 minutes, until the topping is
golden brown and bubbling. Serve
immediately, garnished with the
flat leaf parsley.

VARIATION

Sliced and sautéed courgettes or
potatoes can be used instead of
the aubergines in this dish.

Aubergine Curry

A simple and delicious way of cooking aubergines, which retains their full flavour.

INGREDIENTS

Serves 4

2 large aubergines, about 450 g/1 lb each

45 ml/3 tbsp oil

2.5 ml/½ tsp black mustard seeds

1 bunch spring onions, finely chopped

115 g/4 oz button mushrooms, halved

2 garlic cloves, crushed

1 fresh red chilli, finely chopped

2.5 ml/½ tsp chilli powder

1 tsp ground cumin

1 tsp ground coriander

1.5 ml/¼ tsp ground turmeric

5 ml/1 tsp salt

400 g/14 oz can chopped tomatoes

15 ml/1 tbsp chopped fresh coriander

sprigs of fresh coriander, to garnish

1 Preheat the oven to 200°C/ 400°F/Gas 6. Brush both of the aubergines with 15 ml/1 tbsp of the oil and prick with a fork. Bake in the oven for 30–35 minutes, until the aubergines are soft.

2 Meanwhile, heat the remaining oil in a saucepan and fry the mustard seeds for 2 minutes, until they being to splutter.

3 Add the spring onions, mushrooms, garlic and chilli and fry for 5 minutes. Stir in the chilli powder, cumin, coriander, turmeric and salt and fry for 3–4 minutes. Add the tomatoes and simmer for 5 minutes.

4 Cut each of the aubergines in half lengthways and scoop out the soft flesh into a bowl. Mash the flesh briefly.

5 Add the mashed aubergine and fresh coriander to the saucepan. Bring to the boil and simmer for 5 minutes or until the sauce thickens. Serve garnished with coriander sprigs.

COOK'S TIP
~

If you want to omit some of the oil, wrap the aubergines in foil and bake in the oven for 1 hour.

Vegetable Korma

*The blending of spices produces a
subtle, aromatic curry.*

INGREDIENTS

Serves 4

50 g/2 oz/4 tbsp butter

2 onions, sliced

2 garlic cloves, crushed

2.5 cm/1 in piece of fresh root
    ginger, grated

5 ml/1 tsp ground cumin

15 ml/1 tbsp ground coriander

6 cardamom pods

5 cm/2 in cinnamon stick

5 ml/1 tsp ground turmeric

1 fresh red chilli, seeded and
    finely chopped

1 potato, peeled and cut into 2.5 cm/
    1 in cubes

1 small aubergine, chopped

115 g/4 oz mushrooms, thickly sliced

115 g/4 oz/1 cup French beans, cut into
    2.5 cm/1 in lengths

60 ml/4 tbsp natural yogurt

150 ml/¼ pint/⅔ cup double cream

5 ml/1 tsp garam masala

salt and freshly ground black pepper

sprigs of fresh coriander, to garnish

poppadums, to serve

2 Add the potato, aubergine and
mushrooms and about 175 ml/
6 fl oz/¾ cup water. Cover the pan,
bring to the boil, then lower the
heat and simmer for 15 minutes.
Add the beans and cook,
uncovered, for 5 minutes.

1 Melt the butter in a heavy-
based saucepan. Add the
onions and cook for 5 minutes,
until soft. Add the garlic and
ginger and cook for 2 minutes,
then stir in the cumin, coriander,
cardamoms, cinnamon stick,
turmeric and chilli. Cook, stirring,
for 30 seconds.

VARIATION

Any combination of vegetables
can be used for this korma,
including carrots, cauliflower,
broccoli, peas and chick-peas.

3 With a slotted spoon, remove
the vegetables to a warmed
serving dish and keep hot. Allow
the cooking liquid to bubble up
until it reduces a little. Season with
salt and pepper, then stir in the
yogurt, cream and garam masala.
Pour the sauce over the vegetables
and garnish with coriander. Serve
with poppadums.

Mushroom and Okra Curry

This simple but delicious curry with its fresh gingery mango relish is best served with plain basmati rice.

INGREDIENTS

Serves 4

4 garlic cloves, roughly chopped

2.5 cm/1 in piece of fresh root ginger, peeled and roughly chopped

1–2 fresh red chillies, seeded and chopped

175 ml/6 fl oz/¾ cup cold water

15 ml/1 tbsp sunflower oil

5 ml/1 tsp coriander seeds

5 ml/1 tsp cumin seeds

5 ml/1 tsp ground cumin

2 green cardamom pods, seeds removed and ground

pinch of ground turmeric

400g/14 oz can chopped tomatoes

450 g/1 lb mushrooms, quartered if large

225 g/8 oz okra, trimmed and cut into 1 cm/½ in slices

30 ml/2 tbsp chopped fresh coriander

For the mango relish

1 large ripe mango, about 500 g/1¼ lb in weight

1 small garlic clove, crushed

1 onion, finely chopped

10 ml/2 tsp grated fresh root ginger

1 fresh red chilli, seeded and finely chopped

pinch of salt and sugar

1 To make the mango relish, peel the mango and cut off the flesh from the stone.

2 In a bowl, mash the mango flesh with a fork or process in a food processor or blender. Mix in the rest of the relish ingredients. Set to one side.

3 Place the garlic, ginger, chillies and 45 ml/3 tbsp of the water into a blender or food processor and process until smooth.

4 Heat the sunflower oil in a large saucepan. Add the whole coriander and cumin seeds and allow them to sizzle for a few seconds. Add the ground cumin, ground cardamom and ground turmeric and cook for about 1 minute more.

5 Add the garlic paste, tomatoes and remaining water. Stir to mix well, then add the mushrooms and okra. Stir again, then bring to the boil. Reduce the heat, cover and simmer for 5 minutes.

6 Remove the cover, turn up the heat slightly and cook for another 5–10 minutes, until the okra is tender but not too soft.

7 Stir in the fresh coriander and serve with the mango relish and rice.

COOK'S TIP

When buying okra, choose firm, brightly coloured pods that are less than 10 cm/4 in long.

Provençal Stuffed Peppers

Stuffed peppers are easy to make for a light and healthy supper.

Serves 4

15 ml/1 tbsp olive oil

1 red onion, sliced

1 courgette, diced

115 g/4 oz mushrooms, sliced

1 garlic clove, crushed

400 g/14 oz can chopped tomatoes

15 ml/1 tbsp tomato purée

40 g/1½ oz/scant ⅓ cup pine nuts

30 ml/2 tbsp chopped fresh basil

4 large yellow peppers

50 g/2 oz/½ cup red Leicester cheese, finely grated

salt and freshly ground black pepper

fresh basil leaves, to garnish

2 Stir in the tomatoes and tomato purée, then bring to the boil and simmer, uncovered, for 10–15 minutes, stirring occasionally, until thickened slightly. Remove from the heat and stir in the pine nuts, basil and seasoning.

3 Cut the peppers in half lengthways and seed them. Blanch in a pan of boiling water for about 3 minutes. Drain.

4 Place the peppers in a shallow ovenproof dish and fill with the vegetable mixture.

5 Cover the dish with foil and bake for 20 minutes. Uncover, sprinkle each pepper with grated cheese and bake for a further 5–10 minutes, until the cheese is melted and bubbling. Garnish with basil leaves and serve.

1 Preheat the oven to 180°C/350°F/Gas 4. Heat the oil in a saucepan, add the onion, courgette, mushrooms and garlic and cook gently for 3 minutes, stirring occasionally.

VARIATION

Use the vegetable filling to stuff other vegetables, such as courgettes or aubergines, in place of the peppers.

Spicy Chick-pea and Aubergine Stew

This is a Lebanese dish that's full of the spicy flavours of the Middle East.

INGREDIENTS

Serves 4

3 large aubergines, cubed
200 g/7 oz/1 cup chick-peas,
    soaked overnight
60 ml/4 tbsp olive oil
3 garlic cloves, chopped
2 large onions, chopped
2.5 ml/½ tsp ground cumin
2.5 ml/½ tsp ground cinnamon
2.5 ml/½ tsp ground coriander
3 x 400 g/14 oz cans chopped tomatoes
salt and freshly ground black pepper

For the garnish
30 ml/2 tbsp olive oil
1 onion, sliced
1 garlic clove, sliced
sprigs of fresh coriander

1 Place the aubergines in a colander and sprinkle them with salt. Sit the colander in a bowl and leave for 30 minutes, to allow the bitter juices to escape. Rinse the aubergine with cold water and dry on kitchen paper.

2 Drain the chick-peas and put in a saucepan with enough water to cover. Bring to the boil and simmer for 1–1½ hours, or until tender. Drain.

3 Heat the oil in a large saucepan. Add the garlic and onion and cook until soft. Add the spices and cook, stirring, for a few seconds. Add the aubergine and stir. Cook for 5 minutes. Add the tomatoes and chick-peas and season with salt and pepper. Cover and simmer for 20 minutes.

4 To make the garnish, heat the oil in a frying pan and, when very hot, add the sliced onion and garlic. Fry until golden and crisp. Serve the stew with rice, topped with the onion and garlic and garnished with coriander.

Vegetable Hot-pot with Cheese Triangles

Use a selection of your favourite vegetables, so long as the overall weight remains the same. Firm vegetables may need a little longer cooking time.

INGREDIENTS

Serves 6

30 ml/2 tbsp oil
2 garlic cloves, crushed
1 onion, roughly chopped
5 ml/1 tsp mild chilli powder
450 g/1 lb potatoes, peeled and
    roughly chopped
450 g/1 lb celeriac, peeled and
    roughly chopped
350 g/12 oz carrots, roughly chopped
350 g/12 oz trimmed leeks, roughly
    chopped
225 g/8 oz brown-cap mushrooms, halved
20 ml/4 tsp plain flour
600 ml/1 pint/2½ cups vegetable stock
400 g/14 oz can chopped tomatoes
15 ml/1 tbsp tomato purée
30 ml/2 tbsp chopped fresh thyme
400 g/14 oz can kidney beans, drained
    and rinsed
salt and freshly ground black pepper
sprigs of fresh thyme, to garnish
    (optional)

For the topping
115 g/4 oz/8 tbsp butter
225 g/8 oz/2 cups self-raising flour
115 g/4 oz Cheddar cheese, grated
30 ml/2 tbsp snipped fresh chives
about 75 ml/5 tbsp milk

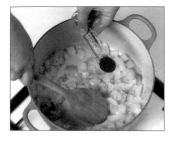

1 Preheat the oven to 180°C/350°F/Gas 4. Heat the oil in a large flameproof casserole and fry the garlic and onion for 5 minutes, or until beginning to brown. Stir in the chilli powder and cook for a further 1 minute.

2 Add the potatoes, celeriac, carrots, leeks and mushrooms. Cook for 3–4 minutes. Stir in the flour and cook for 1 minute.

3 Gradually stir in the stock with the tomatoes, tomato purée, thyme and season with plenty of salt and pepper. Bring to the boil, stirring. Cover and cook in the oven for 30 minutes.

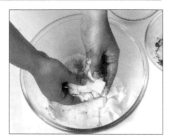

4 Meanwhile, make the topping. Rub the butter into the flour, stir in half the cheese with the chives and plenty of salt and pepper. Add just enough milk to make a smooth dough.

5 Roll out the dough until it is 2.5 cm/1 in thick. Cut into 12 triangles and brush with milk.

6 Remove the casserole from the oven, add the beans and stir to combine. Place the triangles on top and sprinkle with the remaining cheese. Return to the oven, uncovered, for 20–25 minutes. Serve garnished with the fresh thyme sprigs, if using.

Sweet and Sour Mixed Bean Hot-pot

*An appetizing mixture of beans and
vegetables in a tasty sweet and sour
sauce, topped with potato.*

INGREDIENTS

Serves 6

450 g/1 lb unpeeled potatoes
15 ml/1 tbsp olive oil
40 g//1½ oz/3 tbsp butter
40 g/1½ oz/⅓ cup plain wholemeal flour
300 ml/½ pint/1¼ cups passata
150 ml/¼ pint/⅔ cup unsweetened
   apple juice
60 ml/4 tbsp each light soft brown sugar,
   tomato ketchup, dry sherry, cider
   vinegar and light soy sauce
400 g/14 oz can butter beans
400 g/14 oz can flageolet beans
400 g/14 oz can chick-peas
175 g/6 oz green beans, chopped
   and blanched
225 g/8 oz shallots, sliced and blanched
225 g/8 oz mushrooms, sliced
15 ml/1 tbsp each chopped fresh thyme
   and marjoram
salt and freshly ground black pepper
sprigs of fresh herbs, to garnish

1 Preheat the oven to
200°C/400°F/Gas 6. Thinly
slice the potatoes and par-boil
them for 4 minutes. Drain the
potatoes thoroughly, toss them in
the oil so they are lightly coated all
over and set aside.

2 Place the butter, flour, passata,
apple juice, sugar, tomato
ketchup, sherry, vinegar and soy
sauce in a saucepan. Heat gently,
whisking continuously, until the
sauce comes to the boil and
thickens. Simmer gently for 3
minutes, stirring.

3 Rinse and drain the beans and
chick-peas and add to the
sauce with all the remaining ingredients, except the herb garnish.
Mix well.

4 Spoon the bean mixture into a
casserole.

5 Arrange the potato slices over
the top, overlapping them
slightly and completely covering
the bean mixture.

6 Cover the casserole with foil
and bake for about 1 hour,
until the potatoes are cooked and
tender. Remove the foil for the last
20 minutes of the cooking time, to
lightly brown the potatoes. Serve
garnished with fresh herb sprigs.

COOK'S TIP

Vary the proportions of beans
used in this recipe, depending on
what ingredients you have in
your store cupboard.

Spicy Jacket Potatoes

Simple baked potatoes take on an exciting new character with the addition of a few herbs and spices.

Serves 2–4

2 large baking potatoes
5 ml/1 tsp sunflower oil
1 small onion, finely chopped
2.5 cm/1 in piece fresh root ginger, grated
5 ml/1 tsp ground cumin
5 ml/1 tsp ground coriander
2.5 ml/½ tsp ground turmeric
garlic salt
natural yogurt and sprigs of fresh
    coriander, to serve

1 Preheat the oven to 190°C/375°F/Gas 5. Prick the potatoes with a fork. Bake for 1 hour, or until soft.

2 Cut the potatoes in half and scoop out the flesh. Heat the oil in a non-stick frying pan and fry the onion for a few minutes to soften. Stir in the ginger, cumin, coriander and turmeric.

3 Stir over a low heat for about 2 minutes, then add the potato flesh and garlic salt, to taste.

4 Cook the potato mixture for a further 2 minutes, stirring occasionally. Spoon the mixture back into the potato shells and top each with a spoonful of natural yogurt and a sprig or two of fresh coriander. Serve hot.

Baked Leeks with Cheese and Yogurt

Like all vegetables, the fresher leeks are, the better their flavour, and the freshest leeks available should be used for this dish. Small, young leeks are around at the beginning of the season and are perfect to use here.

INGREDIENTS

Serves 4

25 g/1 oz/2 tbsp butter
8 small leeks, about 675 g/1½ lb
2 small eggs or 1 large one, beaten
150 g/5 oz fresh goat's cheese
85 ml/3 fl oz/⅓ cup natural yogurt
50 g/2 oz Parmesan cheese, grated
25 g/1 oz/½ cup fresh white or brown
   breadcrumbs
salt and freshly ground black pepper

1 Preheat the oven to 180°C/350°F/Gas 4. Butter a shallow ovenproof dish. Trim the leeks, cut a slit from top to bottom and rinse well under cold water.

2 Place the leeks in a saucepan of water, bring to the boil and simmer gently for 6–8 minutes, until just tender. Remove and drain well using a slotted spoon. Arrange in the prepared dish.

3 Beat the eggs with the goat's cheese, yogurt and half the Parmesan cheese. Season well with salt and pepper.

4 Pour the cheese and yogurt mixture over the leeks. Mix the breadcrumbs and remaining Parmesan cheese together and sprinkle over the sauce. Bake for 35–40 minutes, until the top is crisp and golden brown.

Tofu Stir-fry with Egg Noodles

Sweet and delicately flavoured, this is the perfect supper for lovers of Chinese food.

INGREDIENTS

Serves 4

225 g/8 oz firm smoked tofu (beancurd)
45 ml/3 tbsp dark soy sauce
30 ml/2 tbsp sherry or vermouth
3 leeks, thinly sliced
2.5 cm/1 in piece fresh root ginger, peeled and finely grated
1–2 fresh red chillies, seeded and sliced in rings
1 small red pepper, seeded and sliced thinly
150 ml/¼ pint/⅔ cup vegetable stock
10 ml/2 tsp runny honey
10 ml/2 tsp cornflour
225 g/8 oz medium egg noodles
salt and freshly ground black pepper

1 Cut the tofu into 2 cm/¾ in cubes. Put it into a bowl with the soy sauce and sherry or vermouth. Toss to coat each piece and then leave to marinate for about 30 minutes.

2 Put the leeks, ginger, chillies, red pepper and stock into a frying pan. Bring to the boil and cook quickly over a high heat for 2–3 minutes, until all the ingredients are just soft.

3 Strain the tofu, reserving the marinade, and set the tofu aside. Mix the honey and cornflour into the marinade.

4 Put the egg noodles into a large pan of boiling water. Remove from the heat and leave to stand for about 6 minutes, until cooked (or follow the package instructions).

5 Heat a non-stick frying pan and quickly fry the tofu until lightly golden brown on all sides.

6 In a saucepan, add the vegetable mixture to the tofu with the marinade and stir well until the liquid is thick and glossy. Spoon on to the egg noodles and serve at once.

VARIATION

Tofu absorbs flavours readily when marinated. If you are not a great fan of tofu, you could substitute it with a firm smoked cheese such as a smoked Bavarian variety, and omit step 5.

Beetroot, Wild Mushroom and Potato Gratin

This inexpensive dish captures the spirit of some of the traditional Polish autumn menus.

INGREDIENTS

Serves 4

30 ml/2 tbsp vegetable oil
1 medium onion, chopped
20 g/¾ oz/3 tbsp plain flour
300 ml/½ pint/1¼ cups vegetable stock
675 g/1½ lb cooked beetroot, peeled
   and chopped
75 ml/5 tbsp single cream
30 ml/2 tbsp creamed horseradish
5 ml/1 tsp hot mustard
15 ml/1 tbsp wine vinegar
5 ml/1 tsp caraway seeds
25 g/1 oz/2 tbsp butter
1 shallot, chopped
225 g/8 oz assorted wild and cultivated
   mushrooms, trimmed and sliced
45 ml/3 tbsp chopped fresh parsley

For the potato border

900 g/2 lb floury potatoes, peeled
150 ml/¼ pint/⅔ cup milk
15 ml/1 tbsp chopped fresh dill (optional)
salt and freshly ground black pepper

1 Preheat the oven to 190°C/375°F/Gas 5. Lightly oil a 23 cm/9 in round baking dish. Heat the oil in a large saucepan, add the onion and fry until soft, without colouring. Stir in the flour, remove from the heat and gradually add the stock, stirring until well blended.

2 Return to the heat, stir and simmer to thicken, then add the beetroot, cream, creamed horseradish, mustard, vinegar and caraway seeds.

3 To make the potato border, bring the potatoes to the boil in salted water and cook for 20 minutes. Drain well and mash with the milk. Add the dill if using and season with salt and pepper.

4 Spoon the potatoes into the prepared dish and make a well in the centre. Spoon the beetroot mixture into the well and set aside.

5 Melt the butter in a large non-stick frying pan and fry the shallot until soft, without browning. Add the mushrooms and cook over a moderate heat until their juices begin to run. Increase the heat and boil off the moisture. When quite dry, season with salt and pepper and stir in most of the chopped parsley.

6 Spread the mushrooms over the beetroot mixture, cover and bake for about 30 minutes. Serve at once, garnished with the reserved parsley.

COOK'S TIP

If planning ahead, this entire dish can be made in advance and heated through when needed. Allow 50 minutes baking time from room temperature.

SPECIAL
OCCASIONS

~

Breaded Aubergine with Hot Vinaigrette

Crisp on the outside, beautifully tender within, these aubergine slices taste wonderful with a spicy dressing flavoured with chillies and capers.

INGREDIENTS

Serves 2

1 large aubergine

50 g/2 oz/½ cup plain flour

2 eggs, beaten

115 g/4 oz/2 cups fresh white
   breadcrumbs

vegetable oil for frying

1 head radicchio

salt and freshly ground black pepper

For the dressing

30 ml/2 tbsp olive oil

1 garlic clove, crushed

15 ml/1 tbsp capers, drained

15 ml/1 tbsp white wine vinegar

15 ml/1 tbsp chilli oil

1 Remove the ends from the aubergine. Cut it into 1 cm/ ½ in slices. Set aside.

COOK'S TIP

It is a good idea to salt the aubergine slices before frying in order to draw out some of their moisture. This will also reduce the amount of oil they absorb.

2 Season the flour with a generous amount of salt and pepper. Spread out in a shallow dish. Pour the beaten eggs into a second dish. Spread out the bread-crumbs in a third.

3 Dip the aubergine slices in the flour, then in the beaten egg and finally in the breadcrumbs, patting them on top to make an even coating.

4 Pour vegetable oil into a large frying pan to a depth of about 5 mm/¼ in. Heat the oil then fry the aubergine slices for 3–4 minutes, turning once. Drain well on kitchen paper.

5 To make the dressing, heat the olive oil in a small pan. Add the garlic and capers and cook over gentle heat for 1 minute. Increase the heat, add the vinegar and cook for 30 seconds. Stir in the chilli oil and remove the pan from the heat.

6 Arrange the radicchio leaves on two plates. Top with the hot aubergine slices. Drizzle over the vinaigrette and serve.

Broccoli Timbales

This elegant but easy to make dish can be made with almost any puréed vegetable, such as carrot or celeriac. To avoid last-minute fuss, make the timbales a few hours ahead and cook while the first course is being eaten. Or serve them on their own as a starter with a little white wine butter sauce.

INGREDIENTS

Serves 4

15 g/½ oz/1 tbsp butter

350 g/12 oz broccoli florets

45 ml/3 tbsp crème fraîche or
    whipping cream

1 egg, plus one egg yolk

15 ml/1 tbsp chopped spring onion

pinch of freshly grated nutmeg

salt and freshly ground black pepper

white wine butter sauce, to serve
    (optional)

fresh chives, to garnish (optional)

1 Preheat the oven to 190°C/375°F/Gas 5. Lightly butter four 175 ml/6 fl oz/¾ cup ramekins. Line the bases with greaseproof paper and butter the paper.

2 Steam the broccoli in the top of a covered steamer over boiling water for 8–10 minutes, until very tender.

3 Put the broccoli in a food processor fitted with the metal blade and process with the cream, egg and egg yolk until smooth.

4 Add the spring onion and season with salt, pepper and nutmeg. Pulse to mix.

5 Spoon the purée into the ramekins and place in a roasting tin. Add boiling water to come halfway up the sides. Bake for 25 minutes, until just set. Invert on to warmed plates and peel off the paper. If serving as a starter, pour sauce around each timbale and garnish with chives.

Fonduta with Steamed Vegetables

Fonduta is a creamy cheese sauce from Italy. Traditionally it is garnished with slices of white truffles and eaten with toasted bread rounds.

INGREDIENTS

Serves 4

assorted vegetables, such as fennel, broccoli, carrots, cauliflower and courgettes
115 g/4 oz/8 tbsp butter
12–16 rounds of Italian or French baguette

For the fonduta
300 g/11 oz/1²⁄₃ cups fontina cheese
15 ml/1 tbsp flour
milk, as required
50 g/2 oz/4 tbsp butter
50 g/2 oz/½ cup freshly grated Parmesan cheese
pinch of grated nutmeg
2 egg yolks, at room temperature
a few slivers of white truffle (optional)
salt and freshly ground black pepper

1 About 6 hours before you want to serve the fonduta, cut the fontina into chunks and place in a bowl. Sprinkle with the flour. Pour in enough milk to barely cover the cheese and set aside in a cool place. The cheese should be at room temperature before being cooked.

2 Just before preparing the fonduta, steam the vegetables until tender. Cut into pieces. Place on a serving platter, dot with butter and keep warm.

3 Butter the bread and toast lightly in the oven or under the grill.

4 For the fonduta, melt the butter in a bowl set over a pan of simmering water, or in a double boiler. Strain the fontina and add it, with 45–60 ml/3–4 tbsp of its soaking milk. Cook, stirring, until the cheese melts. When it is hot, and has formed a homogeneous mass, add the Parmesan and stir until melted. Season with nutmeg, salt and pepper.

5 Remove from the heat and immediately beat in the egg yolks, which have previously been passed through a sieve. Spoon into warmed individual serving bowls, garnish with white truffle, if using, and serve with the vegetables and toasted bread.

Red Pepper and Watercress Filo Parcels

Peppery watercress combines well with sweet red pepper in these crisp little parcels.

INGREDIENTS

Makes 8

3 red peppers
175 g/6 oz watercress
225 g/8 oz/1 cup ricotta cheese
50 g/2 oz/¼ cup blanched almonds,
    toasted and chopped
8 sheets filo pastry
30 ml/2 tbsp olive oil
salt and freshly ground black pepper
green salad, to serve

3 Gradually mix in the ricotta and almonds, and season with salt and pepper.

5 Carefully place 1 of the small squares in the centre of the star shape. Brush lightly with olive oil and top with the second small square.

1 Preheat the oven to 190°C/375°F/Gas 5. Place the peppers under a hot grill until blistered and charred. Place in a paper bag. When cool enough to handle, peel, seed and pat dry on kitchen paper.

4 Working with 1 sheet of filo pastry at a time, cut out 2 x 18 cm/7 in and 2 x 5 cm/2 in squares from each sheet. Brush 1 of the large squares with a little olive oil and place the second large square at an angle of 90° to form a star shape.

6 Top with ⅛ of the red pepper mixture. Bring the edges of the pastry together to form a purse shape and twist to seal. Place on a lightly greased baking sheet and cook for 25–30 minutes, until crisp and golden. Serve with green lettuce.

2 Place the peppers and watercress in a food processor and pulse until coarsely chopped. Spoon into a bowl.

COOK'S TIP

Keep filo pastry refrigerated until you need to use it. When working with the pastry, try to handle it as little as possible and keep the work area cool.

Buckwheat Blinis with Mushroom Caviar

These little Russian pancakes are traditionally served with fish roe caviar and soured cream. The term caviar is also given to fine vegetable mixtures called ikry. This wild mushroom ikry has a rich and silky texture.

INGREDIENTS

Serves 4

115 g/4 oz/1 cup strong white bread flour
50 g/2 oz/¹⁄₃ cup buckwheat flour
2.5 ml/½ tsp salt
300 ml/½ pint/1¹⁄₄ cups milk
5 ml/1 tsp dried yeast
2 eggs, separated
200 ml/7 fl oz/⁷⁄₈ cup soured cream or
  crème fraîche, to serve

For the caviar

350 g/12 oz assorted wild mushrooms,
  such as field mushrooms, orange birch
  bolete, bay boletus, oyster and
  St George's mushrooms
5 ml/1 tsp celery salt
30 ml/2 tbsp walnut oil
15 ml/1 tbsp lemon juice
45 ml/3 tbsp chopped fresh parsley
freshly ground black pepper

1 To make the caviar, trim and chop the mushrooms and place them in a glass bowl. Toss with the celery salt and cover with a weighted plate.

2 Leave the mushrooms for 2 hours, until the juices have run out into the bottom of the bowl. Rinse them thoroughly to remove the salt.

3 Drain and press out as much liquid as you can with the back of a spoon. Return them to the bowl and toss with the walnut oil, lemon juice and parsley. Season with pepper and chill until ready to serve.

4 Sift the two flours together with the salt in a large mixing bowl. Warm the milk to approximately blood temperature. Add the yeast, stirring until dissolved, then pour into the flour. Add the egg yolks and stir to make a smooth batter. Cover with a damp cloth and leave in a warm place to rise, for about 30 minutes.

5 Whisk the egg whites in a clean bowl until stiff, then fold into the risen batter.

6 Heat an iron pan to moderate temperature. Moisten with oil, then drop spoonfuls of the batter on to the surface, turn them over and cook briefly on the other side. Spoon on the mushroom caviar and serve with the soured cream.

Greek Filo Twists

Spinach and feta cheese make up the secret filling hidden inside these pretty filo parcels.

Serves 4

15 ml/1 tbsp olive oil

1 small onion, finely chopped

275 g/10 oz fresh spinach, stalks removed

50 g/2 oz/4 tbsp butter, melted

4 sheets filo pastry (about 45 x 25 cm/
18 x 10 in)

1 egg

pinch of grated nutmeg

75 g/3 oz/¼ cup crumbled feta cheese

15 ml/1 tbsp freshly grated Parmesan
cheese

salt and freshly ground black pepper

1 Preheat the oven to 190°C/375°F/Gas 5. Heat the oil in a pan, add the onion and fry gently for 5–6 minutes, until softened.

2 Add the spinach leaves and cook, stirring, until the spinach has wilted and some of the liquid has evaporated. Leave to cool.

3 Brush four 10 cm/4 in diameter loose-based tartlet tins with a little melted butter. Take two sheets of the filo pastry and cut each into eight 12 cm/4½ in squares. Keep the remaining sheets covered.

4 Brush four squares at a time with melted butter. Line the first tartlet tin with one square, gently easing it into the base and up the sides. Leave the edges overhanging.

5 Lay the remaining three buttered squares on top of the first, turning them so the corners form a star shape. Repeat for the remaining tartlet tins.

6 Beat the egg with the nutmeg and season with salt and pepper. Stir in the cheeses and spinach. Divide the mixture between the tins and smooth the tops. Fold the overhanging pastry back over the filling.

7 Cut one of the remaining sheets of pastry into eight 10 cm/4 in rounds. Brush with butter and place two on top of each tartlet. Press around the edges to seal. Brush the remaining sheet of pastry with butter and cut into strips. Twist each strip and lay on top of the tartlets. Leave to stand for 5 minutes, then bake for 30–35 minutes. Serve hot or cold.

Grilled Vegetable Terrine

Impress your guests with a colourful layered terrine using a mixture of Mediterranean vegetables.

INGREDIENTS

Serves 6

2 large red peppers, quartered, cored
   and seeded
2 large yellow peppers, quartered, cored
   and seeded
1 large aubergine, sliced lengthways
2 large courgettes, sliced lengthways
90 ml/6 tbsp olive oil
1 large red onion, thinly sliced
75 g/3 oz/½ cup raisins
15 ml/1 tbsp tomato purée
15 ml/1 tbsp red wine vinegar
400 ml/14 fl oz/1⅔ cups tomato juice
15 g/½ oz/2 tbsp vegetarian gelatine
fresh basil leaves, to garnish

For the dressing
90 ml/6 tbsp olive oil
30 ml/2 tbsp red wine vinegar
salt and freshly ground black pepper

1 Place the peppers skin side up under a hot grill and cook until blackened. Put in a bowl. Cover.

2 Arrange the aubergine and courgette slices on separate baking sheets. Brush them with oil and cook under the grill.

3 Heat the remaining olive oil in a frying pan. Add the onion, raisins, tomato purée and red wine vinegar. Cook until soft.

4 Line a 1.75 litre/3 pint/7½ cup terrine with clear film.

5 Pour half the tomato juice into a saucepan. Sprinkle with the gelatine. Dissolve over a low heat.

6 Layer the red peppers in the terrine, and cover with some of the tomato juice and gelatine. Add the aubergine, courgettes, yellow peppers and onion mixture.

7 Pour tomato juice over each layer of vegetables and finish with another layer of red peppers.

8 Add the remaining tomato juice to any left in the pan and pour into the terrine. Give the terrine a sharp tap, to disperse the juice. Cover and chill in the refrigerator until set.

9 To make the dressing, whisk together the oil and vinegar. Season with salt and pepper.

10 Turn out the terrine and remove the clear film. Serve in thick slices, drizzled with dressing. Garnish with basil leaves.

Leek Soufflé

Soufflés are a great way to impress guests at a dinner party. This one is simple to make but it looks very sophisticated.

INGREDIENTS

Serves 2–3

15 g/½ oz/1 tbsp butter
15 ml/1 tbsp sunflower oil
40 g/1½ oz/3 tbsp butter
2 leeks, thinly sliced
about 300 ml/½ pint/1¼ cups milk
25 g/1 oz/¼ cup plain flour
4 eggs, separated
75 g/3 oz Gruyère or Emmenthal
    cheese, grated
salt and freshly ground black pepper

1 Preheat the oven to 180°C/350°F/Gas 4. Butter a large soufflé dish. Heat the sunflower oil and 15 g/½ oz/1 tbsp of the butter in a small saucepan or flameproof casserole and fry the leeks over gentle heat for 4–5 minutes, until soft but not brown.

2 Stir in the milk and bring to the boil. Cover and simmer for 4–5 minutes, until the leeks are tender. Strain the liquid through a sieve into a measuring jug.

3 Melt the remaining butter, stir in the flour and cook for 1 minute. Remove from the heat.

4 Make up the reserved liquid with milk to 300 ml/½ pint/1¼ cups. Gradually stir in the milk to make a smooth sauce. Return to the heat and bring to the boil, stirring. When thickened, remove from the heat. Cool slightly and beat in the egg yolks, cheese and leeks.

5 Whisk the egg whites until stiff and, using a large metal spoon, fold into the leek and egg mixture. Pour into the prepared soufflé dish and bake for about 30 minutes, until puffed and golden brown. Serve immediately.

Broccoli and Chestnut Terrine

Served hot or cold, this versatile terrine is equally suitable for a dinner party or for a picnic. A light salad makes an ideal accompaniment.

INGREDIENTS

Serves 4–6

450 g/1 lb broccoli, cut into small florets
225 g/8 oz cooked chestnuts, roughly chopped
50 g/2 oz/1 cup fresh wholemeal breadcrumbs
60 ml/4 tbsp natural yogurt
30 ml/2 tbsp finely grated Parmesan cheese
2 eggs, beaten
pinch of grated nutmeg
salt and freshly ground black pepper
new potatoes, to serve

For the salad and dressing (optional)
60 ml/4 tbsp olive oil
15 ml/1 tbsp lemon juice
2.5 ml/½ tsp caster sugar
salt and freshly ground black pepper
15 ml/1 tbsp chopped fresh thyme or dill
250 g/9 oz mixed green salad leaves

1 Preheat the oven to 180°C/350°F/Gas 4. Line a 900 g/2 lb loaf tin with non-stick baking parchment.

2 Blanch or steam the broccoli for 3–4 minutes, until just tender. Drain well. Reserve ¼ of the smallest florets and chop the rest finely.

3 Mix together the chestnuts, breadcrumbs, yogurt and Parmesan. Season with salt, pepper and nutmeg.

4 Gradually fold in the chopped broccoli, reserved florets and the beaten eggs.

5 Spoon the broccoli mixture into the prepared tin.

6 Place in a roasting tin and pour in boiling water to come halfway up the sides of the loaf tin. Bake for 20–25 minutes.

7 Meanwhile, to make the salad dressing, if using, mix together the olive oil, lemon juice and sugar. Season with salt and pepper and stir in the thyme or dill. Arrange the salad leaves on a plate. Pour the dressing over the salad.

8 Remove the roasting tin from the oven and tip out on to a plate or tray. Cut into even slices and serve with new potatoes.

Goat's Cheese Soufflé

Make sure everyone is seated before the soufflé comes out of the oven because it will begin to deflate almost immediately. The recipe works equally well with strong blue cheeses such as Roquefort.

Serves 4–6

40 g/1½ oz/3 tbsp butter
25 g/1 oz/¼ cup plain flour
175 ml/6 fl oz/¾ cup milk
1 bay leaf
freshly grated nutmeg
grated Parmesan cheese, for sprinkling
40 g/1½ oz herb and garlic soft cheese
150 g/5 oz firm goat's cheese, diced
6 egg whites, at room temperature
1.5 ml/¼ tsp cream of tartar
salt and freshly ground black pepper

1 Melt 25 g/1 oz/2 tbsp butter in a heavy saucepan over medium heat. Add the flour and cook until golden, stirring occasionally.

2 Pour in half the milk, stirring vigorously until smooth. Stir in the remaining milk and add the bay leaf. Season with a pinch of salt and plenty of pepper and nutmeg. Reduce the heat to medium low, cover and simmer gently for about 5 minutes, stirring occasionally.

3 Preheat the oven to 190°C/375°F/Gas 5. Generously butter a 1.5 litre/2½ pint/6¼ cup soufflé dish and sprinkle with Parmesan cheese.

4 Remove the sauce from the heat and discard the bay leaf. Stir in both cheeses.

5 In a clean greasefree bowl, using an electric mixer or balloon whisk, beat the egg whites slowly until they become frothy. Add the cream of tartar, increase the speed and continue beating until they form soft peaks, then stiffer peaks that just flop over a little at the top.

6 Stir a spoonful of beaten egg whites into the cheese sauce to lighten it, then pour the cheese sauce over the remaining whites. Using a large metal spoon, gently fold the sauce into the whites until the mixtures are just combined.

7 Pour the soufflé mixture into the prepared dish and bake for 25–30 minutes, until puffed and golden brown. Serve at once.

Celeriac and Blue Cheese Roulade

Celeriac adds a delicate and subtle flavour to this attractive dish.

Serves 6

15 g/½ oz/1 tbsp butter

225 g/8 oz cooked spinach, drained
   and chopped

150 ml/¼ pint/⅔ cup single cream

4 large eggs, separated

15 g/½ oz Parmesan cheese, grated

pinch of nutmeg

salt and freshly ground black pepper

For the filling

225 g/8 oz celeriac

lemon juice

75 g/3 oz St Agur cheese

115 g/4 oz fromage frais

1 Preheat the oven to 200°C/400°F/Gas 6. Line a 33 x 23 cm/13 x 9 in Swiss roll tin with non-stick baking parchment.

2 Melt the butter in a saucepan and add the spinach. Cook until all the liquid has evaporated. Remove the pan from the heat. Stir in the cream, egg yolks, Parmesan and nutmeg. Season.

3 Whisk the egg whites until stiff, fold them gently into the spinach mixture and then spoon into the prepared tin. Spread the mixture evenly and use a palette knife to smooth the surface.

4 Bake for 10–15 minutes, until the roulade is firm to the touch. Turn out on to a sheet of greaseproof paper and peel away the lining paper. Roll up the roulade with the greaseproof paper inside and leave to cool slightly.

5 To make the filling, peel the celeriac and grate it into a bowl. Sprinkle with lemon juice to taste. Blend the St Agur cheese and fromage frais together and mix with the celeriac and a little black pepper.

6 Unroll the roulade, spread with the filling and roll up again, this time without the paper. Serve at once or wrap loosely and chill.

Spinach and Wild Mushroom Soufflé

Wild mushrooms combine especially well with eggs and spinach in this sensational soufflé. Almost any combination of mushrooms can be used for this recipe, although the firmer varieties provide the best texture for this dish.

INGREDIENTS

Serves 4

225 g/8 oz fresh spinach, washed, or
   115 g/4 oz frozen chopped spinach

50 g/2 oz/4 tbsp unsalted butter, plus
   extra for greasing

1 garlic clove, crushed

175 g/6 oz assorted wild mushrooms such
   as ceps, bay boletuś, saffron milk-caps,
   oyster, field and Caesar's mushrooms

200 ml/7 fl oz/⁷⁄₈ cup milk

20 g/³⁄₄ oz/3 tbsp plain flour

6 eggs, separated

pinch of grated nutmeg

25 g/1 oz Parmesan cheese, grated

salt and freshly ground black pepper

1 Preheat the oven to 190°C/375°F/Gas 5. Steam the spinach over moderate heat for 3–4 minutes. Cool under running water, then drain. Press out as much liquid as you can with the back of a large spoon and chop finely. If using frozen spinach, defrost and prepare following the package instructions. Squeeze dry in the same way.

2 Melt the butter in a saucepan and cook the garlic and mushrooms over low heat until softened. Turn up the heat and evaporate the juices. When dry, add the spinach and transfer to a bowl. Cover and keep warm.

3 Measure 45 ml/3 tbsp of the milk into a bowl. Bring the remainder to the boil. Stir the flour and egg yolks into the cold milk in the bowl and blend well. Stir the boiling milk into the egg and flour mixture, return to the pan and simmer to thicken. Add the spinach mixture to the pan. Season with salt, pepper and nutmeg.

4 Butter a 900 ml/1½ pint/ 3¾ cup soufflé dish, paying particular attention to the sides. Sprinkle with a little of the Parmesan. Set aside.

5 Whisk the egg whites until stiff. Bring the spinach mixture back to the boil. Stir in a spoonful of beaten egg white, then fold the mixture into the remaining egg white.

6 Turn the mixture into the soufflé dish, spread level, scatter with the remaining cheese and bake in the oven for about 25 minutes, until puffed and golden brown. Serve immediately, before the soufflé has a chance to deflate.

COOK'S TIP

The soufflé base can be prepared up to 12 hours in advance and reheated before the beaten egg whites are folded in.

Sweet Potato Roulade

Sweet potato works particularly well as the base for this roulade. Serve in thin slices for a truly impressive dinner party dish.

INGREDIENTS

Serves 6

225 g/8 oz/1 cup low-fat soft cheese

75 ml/5 tbsp natural yogurt

6–8 spring onions, finely chopped

30 ml/2 tbsp chopped brazil nuts, roasted

450 g/1 lb sweet potatoes, peeled and cubed

12 allspice berries, crushed

4 eggs, separated

50 g/2 oz/¼ cup finely grated Edam cheese

15 ml/1 tbsp sesame seeds

salt and freshly ground black pepper

green salad, to serve

1 Preheat the oven to 200°C/400°F/Gas 6. Grease and line a 33 x 25 cm/13 x 10 in Swiss roll tin with non-stick baking parchment, snipping the corners with scissors to fit.

COOK'S TIP

Choose the orange-fleshed variety of sweet potato for the most striking colour.

2 In a small bowl, mix together the soft cheese, yogurt, spring onions and brazil nuts. Set aside.

3 Boil or steam the sweet potato until tender. Drain well. Place in a food processor with the allspice and blend until smooth. Spoon into a bowl and stir in the egg yolks and Edam. Season with salt and pepper.

4 Whisk the egg whites until stiff but not dry. Fold ⅓ of the egg whites into the sweet potatoes to lighten the mixture before gently folding in the rest.

5 Pour into the prepared tin, tipping it to get the mixture right into the corners. Smooth gently with a palette knife and bake for 10–15 minutes.

6 Meanwhile, lay a large sheet of greaseproof paper on a clean dish towel and sprinkle with the sesame seeds. When the roulade is cooked, tip it on to the paper, trim the edges and roll it up. Leave to cool. When cool, carefully unroll, spread with the cheese filling and roll up again. Cut into slices and serve with a green salad.

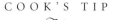

Asparagus Tart with Ricotta

A delightful tart filled with the delicate flavours of mixed cheeses and fresh asparagus.

Serves 4

75 g/3 oz/6 tbsp butter
175 g/6 oz/1½ cups plain flour
pinch of salt

For the filling

225 g/8 oz asparagus
2 eggs, beaten
225 g/8 oz ricotta cheese
30 ml/2 tbsp Greek yogurt
40 g/1½ oz Parmesan cheese, grated
salt and freshly ground black pepper

1 Preheat the oven to 200°C/400°F/Gas 6. Rub the butter into the flour and salt. Stir in enough cold water to form a smooth dough and knead lightly on a floured surface.

2 Roll out the pastry and line a 23 cm/9 in flan ring. Press firmly into the tin and prick all over with a fork. Bake for about 10 minutes, until the pastry is firm but still pale. Remove from the oven and reduce the temperature to 180°C/350°F/Gas 4.

3 Trim the asparagus if necessary. Cut 5 cm/2 in from the tops and chop the remaining stalks into 2.5 cm/1 in pieces.

4 Add the stalks to boiling water and then the asparagus tips. Simmer for 4–5 minutes. Drain.

5 Beat together the eggs, ricotta, yogurt and Parmesan. Season, stir in the asparagus stalks and pour into the pastry case. Place the tips on top. Bake for 35–40 minutes, until golden. Serve warm or cold.

Asparagus with Tarragon Hollandaise

This is the perfect starter for an early summer dinner party, when the new season's asparagus is just in and at its best. Making hollandaise sauce in a blender or food processor is incredibly easy and virtually foolproof!

Serves 4

500 g/1¼ lb fresh asparagus

For the hollandaise sauce

2 egg yolks
15 ml/1 tbsp lemon juice
115 g/4 oz/8 tbsp butter
10 ml/2 tsp finely chopped fresh tarragon
salt and freshly ground black pepper

1 Prepare the asparagus, lay it in a steamer or in an asparagus kettle and place over a saucepan of rapidly boiling water. Cover and steam for 6–10 minutes, until tender (the cooking time will depend on the thickness of the asparagus stems).

2 To make the hollandaise sauce, place the egg yolks and lemon juice in a blender or food processor. Season with salt and pepper and process briefly. Melt the butter in a small pan until foaming and then, with the blender or food processor running, pour it on to the egg mixture in a slow and steady stream.

3 Stir in the tarragon by hand or process it (for a sauce speckled with green or a pale green sauce, respectively).

4 Arrange the asparagus on small plates, pour over some of the hollandaise sauce and sprinkle with pepper. Serve the remaining sauce in a jug.

Spring Vegetable Boxes with Pernod Sauce

Pernod is the perfect companion for the tender taste of early vegetables in crisp cases. This is a very impressive dish for a dinner party and it tastes as good as it looks.

INGREDIENTS

Serves 4

225 g/8 oz puff pastry, defrosted
   if frozen
15 ml/1 tbsp freshly grated
   Parmesan cheese
15 ml/1 tbsp chopped fresh parsley
beaten egg to glaze
175 g/6 oz podded broad beans
115 g/4 oz baby carrots, scraped
4 baby leeks, cleaned
75 g/3 oz/generous ½ cup peas,
   defrosted if frozen
50 g/2 oz mangetouts, trimmed
salt and freshly ground black pepper
sprigs of fresh dill, to garnish

For the sauce
200 g/7 oz can chopped tomatoes
25 g/1 oz/2 tbsp butter
25 g/1 oz/2 tbsp plain flour
pinch of sugar
45 ml/3 tbsp chopped fresh dill
300 ml/½ pint/1¼ cups water
15 ml/1 tbsp Pernod

1 Preheat the oven to 220°C/425°F/Gas 7. Lightly grease a baking sheet.

2 Roll out the pastry very thinly. Sprinkle the grated cheese and parsley over the surface of the pastry sheets, fold and roll once more so that the cheese and parsley are mixed into the pastry. Cut into four 7.5 x 10 cm/ 3 x 4 in rectangles.

3 Lift the rectangles on to the baking sheet. With a sharp knife, cut an inner rectangle about 1 cm/½ in from the edge of the pastry, cutting halfway through. This will be removed once the boxes are cooked. Score criss-cross lines on top of the inner rectangle, brush with egg and bake for 12–15 minutes, until golden.

4 Meanwhile, make the sauce. Press the tomatoes through a sieve into a pan, add the remaining ingredients and bring to the boil, stirring all the time. Lower the heat and simmer until required. Season with salt and pepper.

5 Cook the broad beans in a pan of lightly salted boiling water for about 8 minutes. Add the carrots, leeks and peas and cook for a further 5 minutes. Then add the mangetouts and cook for 1 minute more. Drain all vegetables thoroughly.

6 Using a knife, remove the notched squares from the pastry boxes. Set them aside to use as lids. Spoon the vegetables into the pastry cases, pour the sauce over, put the pastry lids on top and serve garnished with dill.

COOK'S TIP

If there is time, chill the pastry boxes for 20 minutes before baking.

Vegetable Kashmiri

This is a delicious vegetable curry, in which a variety of fresh mixed vegetables are cooked in a spicy, aromatic yogurt sauce.

INGREDIENTS

Serves 4

10 ml/2 tsp cumin seeds

8 black peppercorns

2 green cardamom pods, seeds only

5 cm/2 in cinnamon stick

2.5 ml/½ tsp grated nutmeg

45 ml/3 tbsp oil

1 fresh green chilli, chopped

2.5 cm/1 in piece of fresh root
  ginger, grated

5 ml/1 tsp chilli powder

2.5 ml/½ tsp salt

2 large potatoes, cut into 2.5 cm/
  1 in chunks

225 g/8 oz cauliflower, broken into florets

225 g/8 oz okra, thickly sliced

150 ml/¼ pint/⅔ cup natural yogurt

150 ml/¼ pint/⅔ cup vegetable stock

toasted flaked almonds and sprigs of fresh
  coriander, to garnish

1 Grind the cumin seeds, peppercorns, cardamom seeds, cinnamon stick and nutmeg to a fine powder using a blender or a pestle and mortar.

2 Heat the oil in a large saucepan and fry the chilli and ginger for 2 minutes, stirring all the time.

3 Add the chilli powder, salt and ground spice mixture and fry for about 2–3 minutes, stirring all the time to prevent the spices from sticking.

4 Stir in the potatoes, cover and cook for 10 minutes over low heat, stirring occasionally.

5 Add the cauliflower and okra and cook for 5 minutes.

6 Add the yogurt and stock. Bring to the boil then reduce the heat. Cover and simmer for 20 minutes, or until all the vegetables are tender. Garnish with toasted almonds and coriander sprigs.

COOK'S TIP
~
This curry tastes good using most vegetables. Try to choose vegetables that have contrasting colours and textures.

Filo Vegetable Pie

This stunning pie makes a never-to-be-forgotten main course.

Serves 6-8

225 g/8 oz leeks
165 g/5½ oz/11 tbsp butter
225 g/8 oz carrots, cubed
225 g/8 oz mushrooms, sliced
225 g/8 oz Brussels sprouts, quartered
2 garlic cloves, crushed
115 g/4 oz/½ cup cream cheese
115 g/4 oz Roquefort or Stilton cheese
150 ml/¼ pint/⅔ cup double cream
2 eggs, beaten
225 g/8 oz cooking apples
225 g/8 oz/1 cup cashew nuts or
    pine nuts, toasted
350 g/12 oz frozen filo pastry, defrosted
salt and freshly ground black pepper

1 Preheat the oven to 180°C/350°F/Gas 4. Cut the leeks in half through the root and wash them to remove any soil, separating the layers slightly to check they are clean. Slice into 1 cm/½ in pieces, drain and dry on kitchen paper.

2 Heat 40 g/1½ oz/3 tbsp of the butter in a large pan and cook the leeks and carrots over medium heat for 5 minutes. Add the mushrooms, sprouts and garlic and cook for another 2 minutes. Turn the vegetables into a bowl and let them cool.

3 Whisk the cream cheese and blue cheese, cream and eggs in a bowl. Season with salt and pepper. Pour over the vegetables.

4 Peel and core the apples and cut into 1 cm/½ in cubes. Add them to the vegetables with the toasted nuts.

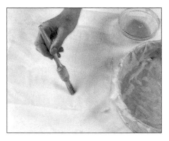

5 Melt the remaining butter in a pan. Brush the inside of a 23 cm/9 in loose-based springform cake tin with melted butter. Brush two-thirds of the filo pastry sheets with butter, one at a time, and use them to line the base and sides of the tin, overlapping the layers so that there are no gaps.

6 Spoon in the vegetable mixture and fold the excess filo pastry over towards the centre to cover the filling.

7 Brush the remaining filo sheets with butter and cut them into 2.5 cm/1 in strips. Cover the surface of the pie with the strips, arranging them decoratively in a rough mound.

8 Bake for 35–40 minutes, until golden brown and crispy all over. Allow to stand for 5 minutes to cool, then carefully remove the cake tin and transfer the pie to a serving plate.

COOK'S TIP

For a firmer crust on the pastry brush the top of the pie with beaten egg just before baking.

Cauliflower and Mushroom Gougère

This puffy, golden-brown, cheese-flavoured case filled with lovely fresh vegetables is a wonderful dinner party dish.

INGREDIENTS

Serves 4–6

115 g/4 oz/8 tbsp butter

150 g/5 oz/1¼ cups plain flour

4 eggs

115 g/4 oz Gruyère or Cheddar cheese, finely diced

5 ml/1 tsp Dijon mustard

salt and freshly ground black pepper

For the filling

1 small cauliflower

1 x 200 g/7 oz can tomatoes

15 ml/1 tbsp sunflower oil

15 g/½ oz/1 tbsp butter

1 onion, chopped

115 g/4 oz button mushrooms, halved if large

sprig of fresh thyme

1 Preheat the oven to 200°C/400°F/Gas 6. Butter a large ovenproof dish. Place 300 ml/½ pint/1¼ cups water and butter together in a large saucepan and heat until the butter has melted. Remove from the heat and add all the flour at once. Beat well with a wooden spoon for about 30 seconds, until smooth. Allow to cool slightly.

2 Beat in the eggs, one at a time, and continue beating until the mixture is thick and glossy. Stir in the cheese and mustard and season with salt and pepper. Spread the mixture around the sides of the ovenproof dish, leaving a hollow in the centre for the filling.

3 Cut the cauliflower into florets, discarding the woody, hard stalk.

4 To make the filling, purée the tomatoes in a blender or food processor and then pour into a measuring jug. Add enough water to make up to 300 ml/½ pint/1¼ cups of liquid.

5 Heat the oil and butter in a flameproof casserole. Fry the onion for 3–4 minutes. Add the mushrooms and cook for 2–3 minutes. Add the cauliflower and stir-fry for 1 minute. Add the tomato liquid and thyme. Season. Cook over low heat for 5 minutes.

6 Spoon into the hollow in the ovenproof dish. Bake for 40 minutes, until the pastry is risen.

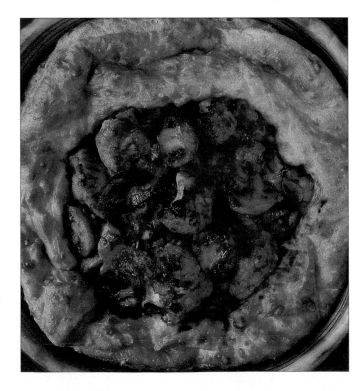

Potato, Spinach and Pine Nut Gratin

Pine nuts add a satisfying crunch to this gratin of wafer-thin potato slices and spinach in a creamy cheese sauce. Serve with a simple lettuce and tomato salad.

INGREDIENTS

Serves 2

450 g/1 lb potatoes

1 garlic clove, crushed

3 spring onions, thinly sliced

150 ml/¼ pint/⅔ cup single cream

250 ml/8 fl oz/1 cup milk

225 g/8 oz frozen chopped spinach, defrosted

115 g/4 oz Cheddar cheese, grated

40 g/1½ oz/scant ¼ cup pine nuts

salt and freshly ground black pepper

lettuce and tomato salad, to serve

1 Peel the potatoes and cut them carefully into wafer-thin slices. Spread them out in a large, heavy-bottomed, non-stick frying pan.

2 Sprinkle the crushed garlic and sliced spring onions evenly over the potatoes.

3 Pour the cream and milk over the potatoes. Place the pan over a gentle heat, cover and cook for 8 minutes, or until the potatoes are tender.

4 Using both hands, squeeze the spinach dry. Add the spinach to the potatoes, mixing lightly. Cover the pan and cook for 2 minutes more.

5 Season with salt and pepper, then spoon the mixture into a shallow, flameproof casserole. Preheat the grill.

6 Sprinkle the grated cheese and pine nuts over the spinach mixture. Heat under the grill for 2–3 minutes until the topping begins to turn golden. Serve with a lettuce and tomato salad.

Spinach and Ricotta Conchiglie

Large pasta shells are designed to hold a variety of delicious stuffings. Few are more pleasing than this mixture of chopped spinach and ricotta cheese.

INGREDIENTS

Serves 4

350 g/12 oz large conchiglie

450 ml/¾ pint/scant 2 cups passata or
    tomato pulp

275 g/10 oz frozen chopped spinach,
    defrosted

50 g/2 oz crustless white bread, crumbled

120 ml/4 fl oz/½ cup milk

60 ml/4 tbsp olive oil

250 g/9 oz/2¼ cups ricotta cheese

pinch of grated nutmeg

1 garlic clove, crushed

2.5 ml/½ tsp black olive paste (optional)

25 g/1 oz/¼ cup freshly grated
    Parmesan cheese

25 g/1 oz/2 tbsp pine nuts

salt and freshly ground black pepper

1 Preheat the oven to 180°C/ 350°F/Gas 4. Bring a large saucepan of salted water to the boil. Toss in the pasta and cook according to the package instructions. Refresh under cold water, drain and reserve until needed.

2 Pour the passata or tomato pulp into a nylon sieve over a bowl and strain to thicken. Place the spinach in another sieve and press out any excess liquid with the back of a spoon.

3 Place the bread, milk and 45 ml/3 tbsp of the oil in a food processor and process. Add the spinach and ricotta and season with salt, pepper and nutmeg. Process briefly to combine.

4 Mix together the passata or tomato pulp, garlic, remaining oil and olive paste, if using. Spread the sauce evenly over the bottom of a flameproof dish.

5 Spoon the spinach mixture into a piping bag fitted with a large plain nozzle and fill the pasta shapes (alternatively, fill with a spoon). Arrange the pasta shapes over the sauce.

6 Heat the pasta through in the oven for 15 minutes. Preheat a moderate grill. Scatter with Parmesan cheese and pine nuts and finish under the grill to brown the cheese.

COOK'S TIP

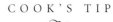

Choose a large saucepan when cooking pasta and give an occasional stir to prevent the shapes from sticking together. If passata is not available, use a can of chopped tomatoes, sieved and puréed.

Index

Apples: red cabbage and apple casserole 200
Artichokes: mixed vegetables with artichokes 200
sweet and sour artichoke salad 80
Asparagus: asparagus rolls with herb butter sauce 55
asparagus soup 26
asparagus tart with ricotta 240
fried noodles, beansprouts and asparagus 116
Spanish asparagus and orange salad 81
with eggs 61
with tarragon hollandaise 240
Aubergines: aubergine curry 204
aubergine dip 44
aubergine, lemon and caper salad 84
aubergine, shallot and tomato calzone 184
breaded aubergine with hot vinaigrette 222
parsnip, aubergine and cashew biryani 170
spicy chick-pea and aubergine stew 209
Szechuan aubergine 106
vegetable moussaka 202
Avocados: fresh spinach and avocado salad 77
guacamole 40

Balti baby vegetables 112
Beancurd see Tofu
Beans: brown bean salad 71
bulgur wheat and broad bean salad 79
frijoles 122
green lima beans in chilli sauce 127
mushroom and bean pâté 53
omelette with beans 162
runner beans with garlic 126
spicy bean and lentil loaf 150
sweet and sour mixed bean hot-pot 212
vegetable chilli 175
white bean soup 25
Beansprouts: fried noodles, beansprouts and asparagus 116

gado gado 156
Beetroot: beetroot and celeriac gratin 125
beetroot, wild mushroom and potato gratin 218
Biryani, parsnip, aubergine and cashew 170
Blinis with mushroom caviar 228

Bolognese, mushroom 178
Bottled and canned goods 16
Bread: mushroom croustades 59
tomato pesto toasties 60
Broccoli: broccoli and cauliflower gratin 131
broccoli and chestnut terrine 232
broccoli and ricotta cannelloni 180
broccoli timbales 224
cauliflower and broccoli with tomato sauce 176
pea, leek and broccoli soup 35
Brown bean salad 71
Brussels sprouts: Chinese 104
festive 105
Buckwheat blinis with mushroom caviar 228
Bulgur wheat and broad bean salad 79
Butter bean, watercress and herb dip 41

Butternut squash and sage pizza 183

Cabbage: gado gado 156
wholemeal pasta with caraway cabbage 176
Calzone, aubergine, shallot and tomato 184
Cannellini beans: white bean soup 25
Cannelloni, broccoli and ricotta 180
Carrots: and coriander soup 31
glazed carrots with cider 130
spiced carrot dip 43
Cashew nuts: parsnip, aubergine and cashew biryani 170
stir-fried vegetables with 141
Cauliflower: broccoli and cauliflower gratin 131
cauliflower and broccoli with tomato sauce 176
cauliflower and mushroom gougère 248
spicy potatoes and cauliflower 94
Celeriac: beetroot and celeriac gratin 125
celeriac and blue cheese roulade 235

Celery soup, curried 32
Ceps with a parsley dressing 160
Cheese: asparagus tart with ricotta 240
aubergine, shallot and tomato calzone 184
baked leeks with yogurt and 215
baked onions stuffed with feta 152
broccoli and ricotta cannelloni 180
butter bean, watercress and herb dip 41
butternut squash and sage pizza 183
celeriac and blue cheese roulade 235
cheese and spinach flan 155
cheese-stuffed pears 58
cheese-topped roast baby vegetables 102
chilli, tomato and spinach pizza 194
filo vegetable pie 246
fonduta with steamed vegetables 225
fried mozzarella 56
goat's cheese soufflé 234
Greek cheese and potato patties 57
Greek filo twists 229
grilled goat's cheese salad 82
leek soufflé 231
onion tarts with goat's cheese 152
Parmesan and poached egg salad 66
pear and pecan salad 68
penne with fennel, tomato and blue cheese 139
potted Stilton with herbs and Melba toast 52
ravioli with ricotta and spinach 186
red pepper and watercress filo parcels 226
ricotta and fontina pizza 198
Roquefort tartlets 63
spinach and ricotta conchiglie 250
summer tomato pasta 134
sun-dried tomato and Parmesan carbonara 161

sweetcorn and cheese pasties
154
sweet potato roulade 238
tagliatelle with spinach
gnocchi 196
tomato and feta cheese salad
83
vegetable hot-pot with cheese
triangles 210
Chestnuts: broccoli and
chestnut terrine 232
festive Brussels sprouts 105
parsnip and chestnut
croquettes 111
Chick-peas: chick-pea falafel
with coriander dip 45
garlic, chick-pea and spinach
soup 23
hummus with pan-fried
courgettes 46
spicy chick-pea and
aubergine stew 209
spicy chick-peas 120
Chilli powder: vegetable chilli
175
Chillies: chilli, tomato and
spinach pizza 194
crispy spring rolls with sweet
chilli dip 50
green lima beans in chilli
sauce 127
rice noodles with vegetable
chilli sauce 142
spicy potato wedges with
chilli dip 49
tofu stir-fry with egg noodles
216
Chinese Brussels sprouts 104
Chinese garlic mushrooms
148
Chinese greens with soy sauce
107
Conchiglie, spinach and
ricotta 250
Coriander ravioli with
pumpkin filling 188
Courgettes: cream of courgette
soup 22
hummus with pan-fried
courgettes 46
split pea and courgette soup
30
with sun-dried tomatoes 128
Couscous salad 70
Croquettes, parsnip and
chestnut 111
Cucumber salad, marinated 75
Curries: aubergine curry 204
curried celery soup 32

curried eggs 62
mushroom and okra curry 206
vegetable Kashmiri 244
vegetable korma 205

Dairy produce 10
Dips: aubergine 44
butter bean and herb 41
chilli 49
coriander 45
guacamole 40
hummus with pan-fried
courgettes 46

saffron 42
spiced carrot 43
Dry goods 14-15

Eggs: asparagus with eggs 61
baked eggs with leeks 147
curried eggs 62
frittata with sun-dried
tomatoes 143
mushroom picker's omelette
163
omelette with beans 162
Parmesan and poached egg
salad 66
purée of lentils with eggs 190
sliced frittata with tomato
sauce 157
sun-dried tomato and
Parmesan carbonara 161

Fajita, vegetable 146
Fennel: fennel, orange and
rocket salad 84

penne with fennel, tomato
and blue cheese 139
Filo parcels, red pepper and
watercress 226
Filo twists, Greek 229
Filo vegetable pie 246
Flan, cheese and spinach 155
Fonduta with steamed
vegetables 225
French onion soup 24
Fresh vegetables 8-9
Frijoles 122
Frittata: sliced frittata with

tomato sauce 157
with sun-dried tomatoes 143
Fritters: hot parsnip fritters on
baby spinach 110
sweetcorn cakes with grilled
tomatoes 159
Fromage frais: saffron dip 42
Fruity rice salad 74
Fusilli with peppers and
onions 136

Gado gado 156
Garlic: Chinese garlic
mushrooms 148
garlic, chick-pea and spinach
soup 23
garlic mashed potatoes 95
garlic mushrooms with a
parsley crust 54
Gazpacho 36
Gnocchi: green gnocchi 144
potato gnocchi 144
tagliatelle with spinach

gnocchi 196
Goat's cheese soufflé 234
Gougère, cauliflower and
mushroom 248
Greek cheese and potato
patties 57
Greek filo twists 229
Greek salad, classic 76
Green lima beans in chilli
sauce 127
Guacamole 40

Harvest vegetable and lentil
casserole 191
Herbs 13
Hollandaise, tarragon 240
Hummus with pan-fried
courgettes 46

Ingredients 8-17

Lasagne, baked vegetable 192
Leeks: baked eggs with creamy
leeks 147
baked leeks with cheese and
yogurt 215
cold leek and potato soup 37
leek, mushroom and lemon
risotto 172
leek soufflé 231
pea, leek and broccoli soup 35
Lentils 11
fresh tomato, lentil and
onion soup 27
harvest vegetable and lentil
casserole 191
purée of lentils with baked
eggs 190
spicy bean and lentil loaf 150
Light lunches 132-63

Mango relish 206
Minestrone with pesto 28
Moussaka, vegetable 202
Mozzarella, fried 56
Mushrooms: beetroot, wild
mushroom and potato
gratin 218
buckwheat blinis with
mushroom caviar 228
cauliflower and mushroom
gougère 248
Chinese garlic mushrooms 148
fresh ceps with a parsley
dressing 160
garlic mushrooms with a
parsley crust 54
leek, mushroom and lemon
risotto 172

mushroom and bean pâté 53
mushroom and okra curry 206
mushroom bolognese 178
mushroom croustades 59
mushroom picker's omelette 163
pepper and wild mushroom pasta salad 72
ricotta and fontina pizza 198
risotto with mushrooms 168
spiced tofu stir-fry 182
spinach and wild mushroom soufflé 236
stuffed mushrooms 151
wild mushroom soup 20

Noodles: fried noodles, beansprouts and asparagus 116
peanut noodles 140
rice noodles with vegetable chilli sauce 142
tofu stir-fry with egg noodles 216
Nut loaf, savoury 149

Okra: mushroom and okra curry 206
tomato and okra stew 129
Omelettes: mushroom picker's omelette 163
omelette with beans 162
Onions: baked onions stuffed with feta 152
classic French onion soup 24
onion tarts with goat's cheese 152
peas with baby onions and cream 123
sweet and sour onions 108
Oranges: fennel, orange and rocket salad 84

Pancakes: buckwheat blinis with mushroom caviar 228
Pappardelle and Provençal sauce 135
Parmesan and poached egg salad 66
Parsnips: hot parsnip fritters on baby spinach 110
parsnip and chestnut croquettes 111
parsnip, aubergine and cashew biryani 170
Pasta: mushroom bolognese 178
wholewheat pasta salad 73
see also Lasagne; Penne etc

Pasta bows, sweet and sour peppers with 78
Pasta primavera 138
Pasta spirals: wholemeal pasta with caraway cabbage 176
Pasties see Pies and pasties
Pâté, mushroom and bean 53
Peanuts: gado gado 156
peanut noodles 140
Pears: cheese-stuffed 58
pear and pecan salad 68
rocket, pear and Parmesan salad 86

Peas: fresh pea soup 34
pea, leek and broccoli soup 35
with baby onions and cream 123
Pecan nuts: pear and pecan salad with blue cheese 68
Penne: summer tomato pasta 134
with fennel, tomato and blue cheese 139
Peppers: fusilli with peppers and onions 136
pepper and wild mushroom pasta salad 72
Provençal stuffed peppers 208
red pepper and watercress filo parcels 226
red pepper risotto 167
roasted potatoes, peppers and shallots 96
spiced tofu stir-fry 182

sweet and sour peppers with pasta bows 78
Pesto: minestrone with 28
tomato pesto toasties 60
Pies and pasties: filo vegetable pie 246
Greek filo twists 229
Pernod sauce, spring vegetable boxes with 242
red pepper and watercress filo parcels 226
sweetcorn and cheese pasties 154

Pilaf, herby rice 102
Pilau, vegetable 166
Pizzas: butternut squash and sage 183
chilli, tomato and spinach 194
ricotta and fontina 198
with fresh vegetables 197
Potatoes: baked sweet potatoes 97
beetroot, wild mushroom and potato gratin 218
cold leek and potato soup 37
garlic mashed potatoes 95
Greek cheese and potato patties 57
potato gnocchi 144
potato, spinach and pine nut gratin 249
potatoes Dauphinois 93
puffy creamed potatoes 92
roasted potatoes, peppers and shallots 96
sautéed potatoes 90

spicy jacket potatoes 214
spicy potato wedges with chilli dip 49
spicy potatoes and cauliflower 94
straw potato cake 90
sweet potato roulade 238
sweet and sour mixed bean hot-pot 212
Provençal stuffed peppers 208
Pulses 11
Pumpkin: coriander ravioli with pumpkin filling 188
pumpkin soup 28

Ratatouille 158
Ravioli: coriander ravioli with pumpkin filling 188
with ricotta and spinach 186
Red cabbage: red cabbage and apple casserole 200
red cabbage in port and red wine 124
Rice: fruity rice salad 74
herby rice pilaf 102
parsnip, aubergine and cashew biryani 170
red fried rice 101
rice with seeds and spices 100
Thai fragrant rice 98
vegetable pilau 166
see also Risotto
Ricotta and fontina pizza 198
Risotto: alla Milanese 174
leek, mushroom and lemon 172
red pepper 167
with mushrooms 168
Rocket, pear and Parmesan salad 86
Roquefort tartlets 63
Roulades: celeriac and blue cheese 235
sweet potato 238
Runner beans with garlic 126

Saffron dip 42
Salads 64-87
artichoke, sweet and sour 80
aubergine, lemon and caper 84
brown bean 71
bulgur wheat and broad bean 79
classic Greek 76
couscous 70
fennel, orange and rocket 84
fresh ceps with a parsley dressing 160

fresh spinach and avocado 77
fruity rice 74
grilled goat's cheese 82
marinated cucumber 75
new spring vegetable 69
Parmesan and poached egg 66
pear and pecan with blue cheese 68
pepper and wild mushroom pasta 72
rocket, pear and Parmesan 86
Spanish asparagus and orange 81
sweet and sour peppers with pasta bows 78
tomato and feta cheese 83
tomato, spring onion and coriander 87
wholewheat pasta 73
Side dishes 88-131
Soufflés: goat's cheese 234
leek 231
spinach and wild mushroom soufflé 236
Soups 18-37
Soy sauce, Chinese greens with 107
Spanish asparagus and orange salad 81
Special occasions 220-51
Spices 12
Spinach: celeriac and blue cheese roulade 235
cheese and spinach flan 155
chilli, tomato and spinach pizza 194
fresh spinach and avocado salad 77
garlic, chick-pea and spinach soup 23
Greek filo twists 229
green gnocchi 144
hot parsnip fritters on baby spinach 110
potato, spinach and pine nut gratin 249
ravioli with ricotta and spinach 186
spinach and ricotta conchiglie 250
spinach and wild mushroom soufflé 236
tagliatelle with spinach gnocchi 196
with raisins and pine nuts 109
Split pea and courgette soup 30

Spring rolls with sweet chilli dip 50
Spring vegetable boxes with Pernod sauce 242
Spring vegetable stir-fry 114
Squash: butternut squash and sage pizza 183
Starters 38-63
Straw potato cake 90
Suppers 164-219
Sweet and sour mixed bean hot-pot 212
Sweet and sour onions 108

Sweet and sour peppers with pasta bows 78
Sweet potatoes: baked sweet potatoes 97
sweet potato roulade 238
Sweetcorn: sweetcorn and cheese pasties 154
sweetcorn cakes with grilled tomatoes 159
Szechuan aubergine 106

Tagliatelle: sun-dried tomato and Parmesan carbonara 161
with spinach gnocchi 196
Tarragon hollandaise, asparagus with 240
Tarts: asparagus tart with ricotta 240
onion tarts with goat's cheese 152
Roquefort tartlets 63
Terrines: broccoli and chestnut 232

grilled vegetable 230
Thai fragrant rice 98
Tofu: Chinese garlic mushrooms 148
spiced tofu stir-fry 182
tofu stir-fry with egg noodles 216
Tomatoes: aubergine, shallot and tomato calzone 184
cauliflower and broccoli with tomato sauce 176
chilli, tomato and spinach pizza 194

courgettes with sun-dried tomatoes 128
fresh tomato, lentil and onion soup 27
frittata with sun-dried tomatoes 143
gazpacho 36
mushroom bolognese 178
pappardelle and Provençal sauce 135
penne with fennel, tomato and blue cheese 139
ricotta and fontina pizza 198
sliced frittata with tomato sauce 157
summer tomato pasta 134
sun-dried tomato and Parmesan carbonara 161
sweetcorn cakes with grilled tomatoes 159
tagliatelle with spinach gnocchi 196
tomato and feta cheese salad 83

tomato and fresh basil soup 21
tomato and okra stew 129
tomato pesto toasties 60
tomato, spring onion and coriander salad 87
Tortillas: vegetable fajita 146

Vegetables: baked vegetable lasagne 192
balti baby vegetables 112
cheese-topped roast baby vegetables 102
deep-fried root vegetables with spiced salt 117
filo vegetable pie 246
fonduta with steamed vegetables 225
gado gado 156
grilled vegetable terrine 230
harvest vegetable and lentil casserole 191
marinated vegetable antipasto 48
minestrone with pesto 28
mixed vegetables with artichokes 200
new spring vegetable salad 69
pasta primavera 138
pizza with fresh vegetables 197
ratatouille 158
rice noodles with vegetable chilli sauce 142
Spring vegetable boxes with Pernod sauce 242
spring vegetable stir-fry 114
stir-fried vegetables with cashew nuts 141
vegetable chilli 175
vegetable fajita 146
vegetable hot-pot with cheese triangles 210
vegetable Kashmiri 244
vegetable korma 205
vegetable moussaka 202
vegetable pilau 166
vegetables Provençal 118

Watercress: red pepper and watercress filo parcels 226
White beans: omelette with beans 162
white bean soup 25
Wholemeal pasta with caraway cabbage 176

Yogurt, baked leeks with cheese and 215

Acknowledgements

*The publishers would like to thank the following for their
contributions to this book:*

RECIPE CONTRIBUTORS

Michelle Berridale-Johnson, Angela Boggiano, Carla Capalbo,
Jacqueline Clark, Carole Clements, Matthew Drennan, Sarah
Edmonds, Joanna Farrow, Christine France, Silvana Franco,
Sarah Gates, Shirley Gill, Shehzaid Husain, Christine Ingram,
Peter Jordan, Manisha Kanani, Elizabeth Lambert Ortiz, Ruby
Le Bois, Lesley Mackley, Sue Maggs, Sallie Morris, Annie
Nichols, Anne Sheasby, Stephen Wheeler, Kate Whiteman,
Elizabeth Wolf-Cohen, Jenni Wright.

PHOTOGRAPHERS

Karl Adamson, William Adams-Lingwood, Edward Allwright,
Steve Baxter, James Duncan, Michelle Garrett, Amanda
Heywood, Janine Hosegood, David Jordan, Patrick McLeavey,
Thomas Odulate, Peter Reilly.

STYLISTS

Madeleine Brehaut, Michelle Garrett, Amanda Heywood,
Clare Hunt, Marian Price, Kirsty Rawlings, Judy Williams.

HOME ECONOMISTS

Hilary Guy, Jane Hartshorn, Wendy Lee, Lucy McKelvie,
Jane Stevenson, Stephen Wheeler.

NOTES

NOTES

NOTES

NOTES

NOTES

NOTES

NOTES

NOTES